Zuzu's Wonderful Life

and other poems

Greg Asimakoupoulos

"Pastor Greg continues to embrace the positive messages from the film, 'It's a Wonderful Life'. Enjoy reading as he shares his nuggets of faith and wisdom."

- Karolyn (Zuzu Bailey) Grimes

"Over the past few years Pastor Greg has become part of my wonderful life. His ability to share God's love through inspirational stories and poetry has blessed me and my family over and over again."

- Carol (Janie Bailey) Coombs Mueller

"The Legend keeps growing...Enough can't be said about 'It's a Wonderful Life's' continued success..."
- Jimmy (Tommy Bailey) Hawkins

"Philosophers have long considered the question, 'Is life worth living?' This book of poems by Greg Asimakoupoulos is a resounding affirmation of life not only being worth living but more importantly, life is wonderful! Thank you, Greg, for reminding us of the wonder of being."

- Jeanine (Young Violet Bick) Roose

I dedicate this book to Star Asimakoupoulos, who first focused my gaze heavenward. Not only did my mom introduce me to God's love, she was my north star giving me a point of reference in my journey through life. I first saw *It's a Wonderful Life* on a date with my mom half a century ago. My guiding Star left my wonderful life through the door of death while I was completing this volume. Peace to her memory!

Acknowledgements

I would like to thank Stephen and Karen Beals for their enduring friendship. Every time I visit Seneca Falls, New York (the Real Bedford Falls), their hospitality reminds me that George and Mary Bailey are more than characters in a classic old movie.

I want to thank gifted illustrator Joe Yakovetic for the book's cover art originally created for a poster version of the poem *Zuzu's Wonderful Life*. His winsome caricatures of the Bailey children capture the spirit of faith, hope and love contained in these pages.

I am also grateful for the editorial assistance of The Reverend Richard Lindholtz. Rick's extensive experience in publishing is a gift to me. His writing and pastoral leadership inspire me.

Mostly I want to thank my wife, Wendy, for her encouragement of me and her celebration of my gifts. Her partnership in ministry over the past four decades has made for a most wonderful life. It's a wonderful life that also includes our three adult daughters Kristin, Allison and Lauren as well as our two granddaughters, Imogen and Ivy (and their gifted father Tim). Hee haw!

Introduction

I first saw *It's a Wonderful Life* on a date with the first love of my life (my mom). The year was 1974. It was a couple weeks before Christmas. I had just graduated from college and started a new job.

As I watched Jimmy Stewart and Donna Reed bring George and Mary Bailey to life, my eyes filled with tears. The values represented in the movie reminded me of the lessons of faith, family and friendship that had been engraved on my life long before I went away to university. I was deeply moved. As a result, watching Frank Capra's classic motion picture has become one of my annual Christmas traditions.

Thirty years after first viewing the film, I met Karolyn Grimes who played Zuzu Bailey in *It's a Wonderful Life*. Karolyn was playing the part of Mary Bailey in a radio drama production of the screen play. Thus began a growing friendship that continues to this day.

At the annual *It's a Wonderful Life* Festival in Seneca Falls, New York, I have been able to get to know and establish relationships with the surviving members of the 1946 cast.

In addition to writing a number of articles about the Bailey kids for periodicals and blog posts, I was invited by a publisher to write a devotional book on the movie in 2012. The result was *Finding God in It's a Wonderful Life.*

Zuzu's Wonderful Life (and other poems) is a sequel to the original volume. It picks up on the inspirational themes of the film through poetry, a genre I have enjoyed for most of my adult life.

Several of the poems contained in this book originally appeared in my weekly poetry blog *Rhymes and Reasons,* accessed at www.partialobserver.com

Most of the poems in this volume conclude with a question or a comment that invites personal reflection and application. My hope is that you will ponder the meaning of the poem and apply it to your life in a tangible way.

Mother Mary, Comfort Me

Like she who birthed the holy child,
the Bailey's mother, calm and mild,
would cradle, nurture, soothe and love
aware of what's at stake.

When daily life refused to rhyme,
George Bailey's wife would find the time
to whisper to her anxious kids
that all would be okay.

This Mary comforted her brood.
She felt their pain. She understood.
She offered hope when all seemed lost.
Her heart was full of grace.

Like Mother Mary, my mom was
a source of comfort just because.
That's who she was. A gentle soul.
A bridge to Father God.

Zuzu's Wonderful Life

and other poems

May your wonderful life
be enriched as you read
where the wonders of true wealth
are found...

in a movie we love,
in the truths of God's Word
and wherever His blessings
abound.

Happy reading!

Pastor Greg

Zuzu's Wonderful Life

The Bailey home claimed four young kids
with Zuzu number three.
But Zuzu didn't mind her place at all.
Her daddy called her Ginger Snap.
She loved that name a lot.
A nickname is a *wonder* when you're small.

And siblings can be *wonders*, too,
especially if they're kind.
In Zuzu's case, they were her closest friends.
Both Pete and Janie helped her learn
and Tommy made her laugh.
Their love for one another knew no end.

Another *wonder* Zuzu claimed
was living in a town
where neighbors cared
for those who were in need.
In Bedford Falls the children played
without concern for fear
and only Mr. Potter dealt with greed.

One other source of *wonder*
was the Bailey's dad and mom.
Both George and Mary were amazing folks.
They gave their sons and daughters
all they needed to succeed.
But Zuzu mostly loved her father's jokes.

Zuzu prayed for her dear daddy
when George got into a jam.
She called on God and Heaven heard her prayer.
And the *wonder* of all *wonders*
is what Zuzu learned that day.
You can share with God your feelings anywhere.

*What concerns crowd your heart today? Why not make
a list of those issues that are too big for you to handle?
As you list your concerns, ask God to intervene.*

It's a Wonderful Life

It's a wonderful life. Every day is a gift.
There's wonder in all that I see.
From a sunrise at dawn
to a moonscape at dusk,
I'm wealthy as wealthy can be.

Refrain:
A wonderful life I've been giv'n.
It's almost like being in Heav'n.
Every day God is near so I've nothing to fear.
A wonderful life He gives me.

It's a wonderful life be it sunshine or rain,
for beauty is found everywhere.
In a spouse's embrace or a grandchild's face,
I treasure these treasures most rare. *Refrain*

It's a wonderful life knowing that I am loved,
that Jesus has died for my sin.
All the guilt and regrets
that once shadowed my past
need never resurface again. *Refrain*

It's a Wonderful Life is much more than a film.
It's a motto that marks how I live.
Because I am blessed
even when things are hard,
I have reason to give and forgive. *Refrain*

tune: Since Jesus Came Into My Heart

*If today is the first day of the rest of your life, what is
one thing you want to make sure you do before you
close your eyes in sleep tonight?*

3

The Gospel According to George Bailey

It's a wonderful life
even though it's been tough
with the hardships and heartaches we've faced.
Our blessings outnumber
what's brought us much pain
as we look back at times we were graced.

It's a wonderful life
if we choose to believe
that our lives have touched others for good.
Through the words that we say
or the deeds that we do,
we bring joy to the world as we should.

It's a wonderful life
we've been given by God.
What George Bailey discovered is true.
Every day is a gift
to unwrap and enjoy
while acknowledging someone needs you.

It's a wonderful life
Christmas Day promises.
A life that goes on when we die.
A life most abundant
where love wins the day
and offers what money can't buy.

A Wonderful Life After All

You've really had a wonderful life.
Amazing kids. An awesome wife.
A job you love and countless friends.
The Lord's been good to you.

Don't say you wish you'd not been born.
In spite of setbacks, trials and storms,
you have been blessed in many ways.
The Lord's been good to you.

Accept each day as Heaven's gift.
Don't let God's daily blessings drift.
It's good to count them every day.
The Lord's been good to you!

Identify five things for which you have to be grateful this week.

Finding God in Bedford Falls

Finding God in Bedford Falls?
By George, I have. Will you?
Like Waldo He keeps showing up
amid the many clues.

He's there at old man Gower's store
and in the Granville home.
You'll find Him there at Harry's prom
or as George prays alone.

He's there beside young Zuzu's bed
and at Martini's bar.
To find the Lord within this film,
you need not look that far.

He's there when Mr. Potter tries
to trap George in his web.
And He is there when George gives up
and wishes he was dead.

Although you'll never see His face,
God's fingerprints abound
within this movie millions love.
The plot is holy ground!

What is your favorite scene in It's a Wonderful Life?

An All-Star Child Star

It's a wonderful life
quite apart from the strife
that we cannot avoid in this world.
Such a claim is the truth
and she is living proof,
looking back to when she was a girl.

"Zuzu Bailey" was blessed
but just who could have guessed
what awaited the young rising star?
Wilted flowers and pain
soon replaced treasured fame.
And although she would heal,
she'd be scarred.

But her scars gave her wings.
She found lyrics to sing
and her petals (once dead) lived again.
She was loved through the night.
Seems that Clarence was right.
No one fails in this life who has friends.

*This poem is dedicated to Karolyn "Zuzu Bailey" Grimes
whose early life was anything but wonderful.*

*Karolyn Grimes is not the only one whose scars turned
to stars. Think about some struggle in your life that
became a stepping stone.*

I Don't Want Plastics

I don't want plastics or any ground floors.
It's love I want.
The George-and-Mary-Bailey kind.
I long for a partnership of co-equals
collaborating in life
with commitment as collateral.

I don't need Sam Wainwright's success
to find fulfillment in what I do.
I need the support of someone
who believes in me
and celebrates my freedom
to follow my dreams
even if those dreams are rooted
in my hometown.

I do not long to just be rich.
I long for the wealth that's found
in another's heart
and the opportunity to deposit
compounding interest
on a daily basis.

Think of someone who has influenced your life for good whose "wealth" is not measured by their financial portfolio.

No Man is a Failure

An inscription in a book declared
a truth that's true most anywhere.
No man's a failure (though he's poor)
if that man has a friend.

Tom Sawyer and his friend Huck Finn
proved what we need to hear again:
A shared joy is a doubled joy.
And sharing pain hurts less.

*Look back on the past decades of your life. Who was
your best friend during each decade? How did you
benefit from their friendship?*

Are You Game, Vi?

Don't let what others choose to do
dictate how you will live.
Unlace your shoes,
take off your socks and climb.
Mount Bedford waits
for those who dare
to let their passions free.
Embrace the world around you
while there's time.

Identify five ways you can "embrace your world" this weekend. You get extra-credit if your answers don't cost money.

The Brother Who Stayed Home

When his brother left for college,
George remained at home to work.
He stayed behind when Harry went to war.
When Marty, Sam and others
moved away to seek their fame,
George found himself
in Bedford Falls once more.

Initially, resentment
could be found in George's heart.
But as time passed
George proved that home was best.
His life was marked by blessings
as he served the common good.
George Bailey was the mark of true success.

Who in your family of origin was most like George Bailey? Do you think they ever felt envious of those who moved away?

Youth is Wasted

Youth is wasted on the young.
We grow too old too fast.
And by the time we want to play
our energy won't last.

And so the moral of it all
is *seize the day* each day.
Awake with wonder from your sleep
and choose to dance today.

Forget how many candles will be on your next birthday cake. What can you do today that reaffirms the fact you are still young at heart?

I Just Can't Imagine

I just can't imagine a world without you.
You fill it with blessings galore.
Your smile, your laughter,
your wisdom and heart
touch my life and so many more.

I just can't imagine a world without you.
You offer what no one else can
in ways that make others
feel special and great.
You are part of God's customized plan.

Text, email, telephone or mail a handwritten note to someone who might not realize just how important they are in your life.

Let George Do It

When Mr. Gower needs to be challenged,
let George do it!
When someone needs to help the Martinis
find an affordable home,
let George do it!
When the Building & Loan needs
a new president,
let George do it!
When an angel needs someone to save him,
let George do it!
When Violet Bick needs a helping hand,
let George do it!

When in doubt,
let George do it!
When others hesitate,
let George do it!
When time is of the essence
let George do it!
When you need some to stand up to evil,
let George do it!
When no one else is willing,
let George do it!
When you wonder what Jesus would do,
let George do it!

By George, don't you want to be like him?
Just do it!

*What random act of kindness can you do for someone in
your sphere of influence?*

My Kind of Town

My kind of town is...

Where the Bijou shows the latest film
and Ernie takes me there.
Where Gower's fountain slakes my thirst
and drowns my every care.

At Martini's you can meet the boys
and order up some beers
while Nick, the tender of the bar,
is quick to offer cheers.

In Bedford Falls I feel at home.
The townsfolk know my name.
My neighbors are my family
and I to them the same.

In what ways was your hometown similar to Bedford Falls?

Ask Dad. He Knows!

Ask Dad. He knows.
He's paid his dues.
And dues pay dividends.
Your old man's learned
by trial and error
how failure is your friend.

So don't be proud.
Admit your need.
Your Father longs to be
a source of help.
But understand!
Requesting is the key.

Make of list of what you need your Heavenly Father to handle on your behalf.

Taking Stock of Your True Wealth

What you give is what you take
when this old life is through.
How generous you choose to be
is simply up to you.

Possessions gather dust and break.
Things fail to satisfy.
But time with others reaps rewards
compounding when we die.

A plaque on George and Mary's wall
reminds us of a key
unlocking ways to serve the poor
through generosity.

It calls us to remember
that the wealth we give away
will constitute our legacy
when we leave earth someday.

The plaque on the Bailey's wall is similar to what martyred missionary Jim Elliot once wrote, "He is no fool who gives what he cannot keep to gain what he cannot lose." Try writing your own paraphrase of that axiom.

Paste It, Daddy!

"Paste it, Daddy, paste it,"
we hear little Zuzu say.
And we think of times our children
voiced their need.
They looked to us for answers
when life dealt them a bum hand
or when (confused) they hoped
we'd take the lead.

It's awesome to be needed
for the time comes way too soon ·
when our children don't require helping hands.
So let's heed those little voices
that call out for paste or glue
and offer "Daddy fixes" while we can.

*Think back to a "Daddy fix" when you were younger.
When did your dad come to the rescue just at the right
time?*

Zuzu's Petals

Dried petals pressed within a book
invite my eyes to take a look
at what recalls a memory
I never will forget.

There was a time my child was sick.
And like a fragile candle wick,
I wondered if the flickering flame
would disappear in smoke.

I asked the Lord to give me grace
not knowing what I'd have to face.
And then I saw a yellow rose
beside my daughter's bed.

It was as if I heard God say,
"That fragrant flower (like today)
is given as a priceless gift.
So cherish while you can.

Enjoy the fragrance. Seize the day!
Embrace your child. And by the way,
no matter what the future holds,
I will be holding you."

A pressed flower? A faded photo? A tea cup? A
miniature cross? What is a tangible item in your home
that calls to mind a "sacred moment" when you
experienced God's presence during a personal ordeal?

Classic Movie Magic

I love an old-time movie
with a plot that's ever-new.
Where hometown heroes sacrifice and lose.
Where ne'er-do-wells gain traction
in their bid to win the day,
but come up short
to those who've paid their dues.

There's Mr. Deeds and Mr. Smith
and Mr. Holland, too.
There's the Bishop's Wife and Chariots of Fire.
But the film that warms my heart the most
concerns the Bailey Clan
whose timeless plot continues to inspire.

List ten movies that comprise your all-time favorites. For fun, try and identify the lead actors in each.

Pottersville

Pottersville is hell on earth.
It's power and greed.
It's bright lights and dark hearts.
It's cheap thrills with a costly price tag.
It's instant gratification
with delayed consequences.
Pottersville is a world in which
George Bailey was never born
(or Jesus for that matter).

As you reflect on Bedford Falls and Pottersville, what significant differences are noteworthy?

A Bert and Ernie Kind of Life

Bedford Falls and Sesame Street
each claim two friends I'd like to meet.
For Bert and Ernie life consists
in serving those in need.

And though each one is quite unique,
the thing they share is what I seek:
To model friendship day by day
through acts of being kind.

They're kind to those who need a friend
or strangers asking them to lend
a helping hand to see them through
an unexpected trial.

I want a Bert and Ernie life
devoid of conflict, stress or strife
where taxi drivers and police
are loved by those they serve.

*Police officers and taxi/Uber drivers are not the safest
professions. Spend a few moments praying for those
who serve others in risky situations.*

Mental Floss for Uncle Billy

He's reached the age where once again
he plays at hide and seek.
His playmates aren't the kids next door,
but facts he tries to speak.
So much of what he once recalled
gets stuck inside his mind.
Like popcorn hulls between his teeth,
some thoughts get caught he finds.
But gratefully it's just a stage.
It's not a total loss.
He'll do just fine if he can find
a string of mental floss.

Who do you know who is dealing with memory loss?
What can you do to remind that person of their value in
spite of what they can no longer remember?

Doing the Swim

When the floor opens up
and you find yourself treading water
in your dancing shoes,
you have a choice.
You can curse the jerk
that opened the floor
or you can do "the swim"
in your dress-up clothes
and make a memory you'll never forget.

When your plans change
without notice
and it feels like
the rug's been pulled out from under you,
don't despair.
Come up for air
and smile at the camera.

Think back to when someone flipped the switch on you leaving you treading water. How did you react? Would you react differently if you could replay that scene? If so, how?

Excuse Me, I Burped

Tommy pulls his daddy's coat.
He pulls his leg.
He makes a joke.
And we all laugh
because we know
"I burped" is Tommy's line.

But we burp, too.
We make mistakes.
Our lines in life make others ache.
Excuses are quite quick to claim.
To say *"I'm sorry"* is hard.

To whom do you owe an apology?

More Than a Movie Mom

The TV wife we loved as kids
was more than Mary's mom.
Yet, Donna Reed's mystique was hardly known.
A feminist, an advocate for justice,
love and peace.
She was far more than simply
Donna Stone.

No cookie baking homemaker,
this actress had an edge
that cut through common cultural taboos.
This Mary Bailey look-alike
who stole Frank Capra's heart
was more than got reported in the news.

This poem is dedicated to Mary Owen, Donna Reed's youngest daughter, who continues to celebrate her mother's multifaceted legacy.

Do a Google search on the actress who played Mary Bailey. What about Donna Reed did you not know previously?

Two Soda Fountain Dreamers

Two soda fountain dreamers
swivel on their stools and drink
through paper straws that channel liquid gold.
These girls dream of young Georgie
and what life with him might be
as they ponder how their future will unfold.

For Mary and for Violet,
a world at war seems safe
as they sit in Gower's Drugstore with ice cream.
What concerns them isn't Europe
or those doughboys bearing guns.
There's a soda jerk who focuses their dreams.

But only one will win the boy
with visions of his own.
Together George and Mary will achieve
what neither could imagine.
Far beyond their wildest dreams,
they'll come to see what fate had up her sleeve.

*When you were a kid, what was your favorite treat at
the local soda fountain?*

A Friend We Never Knew

As evening fell last night,
the church bells of Bedford Falls
rang out the news
we knew would one day come.
The wonderful life
of one George Bailey
had at long last passed.
At last he has his wings
(I mean to say he grasped
the reward of his faith).
And while Heaven sings
to welcome this child of God,
movie-goers the world over
are mourning the loss
of a friend they never knew.
This tall, lanky, likeable lad,
who stuttered his way into our hearts,
acted with uncanny eloquence and charm.
Some called him Jimmy.
To others he was James.
I think his dear wife called him Jim.
But to folks like me
(inspired by his most memorable role),
Jimmy Stewart will always be George.
And though I never knew him,
I will miss him.
Peace to his memory!

This poem was written in response to Jimmy Stewart's death on July 2, 1997

Mr. Gower, I Feel Your Pain

Mr. Gower, I feel your pain.
Grieving with no one to blame
except the flu that claimed your son.
Your one and only child.

The monster whom we know as grief
is haunting you without relief.
He follows you both night and day.
And mocks your feeble faith.

I cannot fully understand
what stalks you in this shadowland.
But I can ask a loving God
to salve your bleeding heart.

He also lost His only Son.
And when it seemed that Death had won,
God proved there's more than meets the eye.
It's called an empty tomb!

*Spend a few moments praying for someone in your life
who is grieving their way through the valley of
shadows.*

320 Sycamore Street

That old abandoned house
is a picture of my life.
I feel empty and unattractive.
Time has vandalized my beauty.
My paint is peeling.
My foundation is cracked.
My joists are loose.

That old house with broken windows
intrigues me, nonetheless.
Perhaps I'm not destined for the wrecking ball
after all.

Lord, help me see what others can't.
Give me eyes of faith
to glimpse a hopeful future.
Even though the front yard's
overrun with weeds,
help me imagine a garden
just waiting to be planted.
Remind me there's a tomorrow to be claimed.
There's a new day just waiting to dawn.
Even at my age, the old Granville House
can become my Bailey Mansion.
What is it they say?
Where there's a will, there's a way.
I'm willing, Lord, to be remodeled.

*Speaking of restoration. What would you like to change
or remodel in your life? What first steps can you take
this week?*

Oh, Daddy!

We all relate to Janie's plight
when George (upset) went off.
A father's pain results in needless hurt.
Hurt people do hurt people.
And the trauma takes a toll,
especially when you're made to feel like dirt.

Sweet Janie, your dear daddy
didn't mean the things he said.
He was stretched beyond his limit.
He just snapped.
Please forgive him and the others
who have bruised your self-esteem
through their careless words
that felt like you'd been slapped.

*Who do you need to forgive for some past wrong that
hurt you deeply?*

Why Sam Wainwright was All Wrong

Hee-haw, Sam!
You made your fortune,
made a name
and made out fine.
But there's something missing
in your well-played hand.

Like old Scrooge,
it seems your heart is focused
on the bottom line alone.
But there's more to life
than corporate goals and plans.
Take your family, for instance.
Have you given them your time?
Or does work demand
the best you have to give?

When your kids have grown and left you,
will your savings satisfy?
Or will you regret
the way you chose to live?

*Examine your current schedule. What can you change
so to be more available to those who need more of your
time?*

In Celebration of Friendship

No one is a failure
if friendship marks their life.
A friend is a key to success.
A friend opens options
from which you can choose.
A friend locks up unneeded stress.

True friends will confront us
when we believe lies.
They care far too much to be still.
And when we are tempted
to give up our dreams,
a friend puts two steaks on the grill.

Think about a time when a friend loved you enough to challenge you or question a decision. What did you learn from that experience?

Won't You Go Home, George Bailey?

Won't you go home, George Bailey?
Won't you go home?
You're richer than you think.
Your wife and children love you.
Your brother, too.
Though life at times can stink.

When you feel suicidal,
take time to pray.
and give your worries to the Lord.
You've no need to blame.
No need to feel your shame.
George Bailey, won't you please go home?

tune: Won't You Come Home Bill Bailey?

Try your hand at creating an acronym for HOME. (For example, Hugs Offer Me Encouragement)

The Magic of Capra

Frankly speaking, Capra knew
that heartstrings could be pulled.
He offered hope against a screen of fear.
Frank scripted heroes who might fail
when tested to the core.
But through their angst
we see their strength appear.

I love to munch Frank Capra's "corn"
when tempted to give in
to lies that seem to question what I'm worth.
Without exception, I'm inspired
with every film I watch.
For God Almighty chose to give me birth.

*Google Frank Capra. How many of his movies have you
seen? Other than IAWL what one is your favorite?*

In Praise of a Counter Culture

A Norman Rockwell painting of
a soda fountain scene I love
depicts a cop in uniform
with someone much like me.

The marble counter and the stools
were once a hangout after school
where I would stop while heading home
to slurp a chocolate malt.

My boyhood haunt was called *The Owl*
where soda jerks with moistened towel
would wipe the fountain counter clean
of spills we kids had made.

The jerks would call us by first name.
They were quite happy when we came.
The Bean Town pub they once called *Cheers*
had nothing on *The Owl.*

And after all these many years
they still serve shakes instead of beers.
It is a landmark in our town
that's often in the news.

It's like the old-time coffee shop
where (just like clockwork) neighbors stopped
to chew the fat and digest news,
to laugh and shed a tear.

The Owl is still the place I go
to reminisce with folks I know
when I return to my hometown
to see my dad and mom.

*This poem is dedicated to Pam and Frank Higgins who
own and operate The Owl Soda Fountain in Wenatchee,
Washington.*

*In most communities the local Starbucks has replaced
the drugstore soda fountain as the gathering place.
What values do you observe at Starbucks that your
church would do well to emulate?*

Every Time I Hear a Bell

Every time I hear a bell,
I'm prone to realize
that someone loved has left their family.
That ringing sound reminds me of
the speed at which time flies.
And just how near
death's dreaded knock may be.

A ringing bell connects the dots
and brings the past to life.
It's all I need to trigger memories.
A chime in church, a trolley bell
or a digital alarm
invites me to embrace death's mystery.

And so I vow to live each day
with purpose (prayerfully).
To focus on the options at my door.
To give myself to tasks at hand
and those who need my help
anticipating what yet lies in store.

"Every memorial service you attend is one closer to your own." With that in mind, what changes do you want to make in your life while you still can?

When the Black Dog Barks

Depression reigns.
The black dog barks.
I smell his putrid breath.
I'm suffocating in despair.
This darkness seems like death.

I'm paralyzed.
I cannot feel.
This zombie state I'm in
finds me devoid of grief or joy.
I'm languishing within.

O God, I'm not the praying sort,
but I confess I'm done.
Please penetrate this blinding fog
with shafts of morning sun.

Depression's grip is strengthened when you try to battle it alone. If you are struggling with clinical depression, tell someone you trust you need help. If you know someone in depression, reach out to them with an open heart and listening ears.

Praying for Mr. Potter

Kids, let's pray for Mr. Potter.
He's such a scrooge.
There's no joy in his world.
The only carol that plays in his head
is *In the Bleak Midwinter.*
As a result he's lonely, lost and sad.
He's a victim of the pain he's known.

Good grief, Lord, he can't be all bad.
Because he was created in Your image,
he's worthy of redemption.
Though he thinks his worth
is in stocks and bonds alone,
help him come to see that true wealth
isn't really found in bank accounts.
Help him understand that people need more
than cold hard cash to warm their hearts.

Who in your personal world reminds you of Mr. Potter?
Try to imagine circumstances in their life that have
shaped their perspective. Ask the Good Lord to begin to
change their bad choices.

A "Dear George" Letter

Dear George,

Even though I wasn't sure
exactly what to say,
I talked to God and spoke your name.
I prayed for you today.

I asked the Lord to give you strength,
to calm you from your stress,
to free you from the things you fear
and bathe your mind with rest.

I asked the Lord to help you
in the uphill days to come.
I asked our precious loving God
to complete what He's begun.

He whispered in the quiet
and He filled my heart with peace.
He said that you are deeply loved
and that His love won't cease.

Love,
Mary

This letter isn't just for George Bailey. What is going on in your life such that Mary could have written this letter to you? Admit your need to the Lord. Ask God for the faith to trust Him.

The Trip of a Lifetime

Reflecting on an uncle's impending journey to Heaven

He's packed his bags
and now awaits
the trip of a lifetime.

It is a journey
for which he has long prepared.
His ticket was prepaid long ago
by a loving (and generous) Friend.

In recent days
he's dreamed about his destination
having read the travel guide
that graphically pictures
an awesome place
that is nothing short of
"out of this world."

For now, though, my Uncle Billy
rests in the waiting room.
He listens for a whistle
and the welcomed squeal
of steel on steel.
He knows that soon
the approaching train
will arrive at the station
and slow to a stop.

The Conductor will at last appear
and announce in words so soft
only he will hear them.
"Heaven.... All aboard."

Uncle Billy (beaming with joy)
will bound up those metal steps
and find his comfortable seat.
In the twinkling of an eye,
he will realize
that he is no longer weary, weak,
confused or sick.

Fully alive and completely well,
he will look out the window
as the train pulls out of Bedford Falls Station
and see a crowd of family, friends and loved-ones
waving goodbye.

"Don't weep for me," he will call out.
"I'm headed home."
"I'll see you soon," he adds, smiling.

But only those with eyes of faith
will be able to read his lips
on the other side
of the moving window.
And brushing tears from their eyes,
they will return his smile.

*Spend some time reflecting on the final days of someone
you love who recently died. How does your faith give
you hope in the midst of your grief?*

Bread, Salt and Wine

Bread, salt and wine
children and time
friendships that bridge us through grief.
Rest while we sleep.
Joy that runs deep.
Silence both lengthy and brief.

These are the true necessities
by which a home is furnished.
These are the blessings
that increase the value
of that which is far more
than just a shelter.

What makes your home more than a shelter? Make a list of the "intangibles" that furnish it with valuables money can't buy.

A House Blessing

Lord, bless this place
that by Your grace
our family now calls home.
Please fill it with all that is
necessary and good.
Food and drink.
Clothing and furnishings.
Art and music.
Memories and dreams.
Laughter and love.
Health and peace.
Please protect it from theft and fire
and tornado and flood.
Through the clouds of sorrow and uncertainty,
would you shine Your rays of comfort and hope?
And, Lord, may the road that leads to our home
be free from relational potholes and debris.
Let it be an unobstructed path
for those You send to enrich our lives.
May the open door of this sanctuary
symbolize our open hearts
that long to care for all who step inside.

Using this poem as an example, write your own house blessing. Consider printing it and hanging it by your front door.

Have Yourself a *Mary* Christmas

Mary made it Christmas
when ol' George was in a jam.
She canvased the community with hope.
The neighbors proved most generous.
Much cash conveyed their love.
That basket filled with money helped them cope.

Yes, Mary "Christmas" Bailey
modeled how to serve in love.
She did what needed doing with a smile.
She saw a need and acted
without fanfare or applause
when her husband faced an economic trial.

May we all be more like Mary
when it comes to taking charge.
Love is best defined by doing what needs done.
Since this time of year finds loved ones
overwhelmed by mounting stress,
let's determine to take charge while having fun.

*If "love is best defined by doing what needs done," how
can you express love to your family today?*

It's a Wonderful Life (Revised)

Have you ever considered
what life would be like
if that Baby had never been born?
Depraved and deprived,
we'd be prisoners of fear
in a world without order or form.

Yes, His wonderful life
taught the world how to love
and gave reason to hope when we die.
It shaped systems and laws
that defend victim's rights
while denouncing society's lies.

It's a wonderful life
with remarkable names
that describe who He always will be.
A wonderful God
who alone can bring peace
to the world He created... and me!

*Have you ever contemplated how the world would be
different if Jesus Christ had never been born? Try
making a list of what wouldn't exist.*

An Advent Hymn

O come Befriender of the lonely soul
and fill their emptiness until it's full.
Stand by the grieving as they weep
and walk with them although their path is steep.
Rejoice, rejoice, our Friend who knows our plight
and be to us a candle in the night.

O come Defender of the working poor
and give them what they need (and then some more).
Provide them with the means and way
to give their children toys with which to play.
Rejoice, rejoice, our only sure defense
and comfort those whose burdens are intense.

O come Redeemer of our nation's wrongs
and fill our hearts with plaintiff, hopeful songs.
Confront the demons that divide
especially hateful prejudice and pride.
Rejoice, rejoice, Redemption's Child, rejoice
and give all those who worship You one voice.

O come Fulfillment of what God has deemed
and satisfy creation's deepest dreams.
Accomplish all that love demands
and bring about the peace that You have planned.
Rejoice, rejoice, Fulfiller of God's heart
as we rejoice and sing "How Great Thou Art."

tune: O Come, O Come Emmanuel

The Longest Night Lament

I hear Bing's dreams of Christmas White.
But on this dreaded longest night,
my world lacks joy. At best, it's bleak.
This Christmas I am blue.

The colors of this holiday
aren't bright and bold. They're brownish gray.
Depression robs my anguished soul
of sights most people see.

And no one seems to understand.
Emotionless, I'm feeling damned
to spend this Christmas feeling lost
but hoping to be found.

O God, although this night is long
remind me of that ancient song
in which You're called Emmanuel.
Please come and ransom me.

This poem is dedicated to those who are struggling with clinical depression as they attempt to endure this holiday season.

Who comes to mind when you read this poem? When is the last time you communicated with them? Consider making a date to share a meal with them.

We Gather as Fam'ly

We gather as fam'ly
with gratitude, thankful
for freedoms our nation
has fought to preserve.
The freedom of worship,
of speech and to protest,
the freedom from fear
and from want so to serve.

We gather as fam'ly
united and trusting
a loving Creator
who cares for our needs.
We own our dependence
on One who shows mercy
to those undeserving
who long to succeed.

We gather as fam'ly
imperfect, forgiving
and loving each other
because we are one.
This day spent together
recalls many mem'ries
reminding us all
of the blessings we share.

Yes, Lord, we are grateful
in spite of the sorrow
that clouds this occasion
because of our grief.
In spite of a place
at the table that's empty,
we feast knowing
our separation is brief.

tune: We Gather Together to ask the Lord's Blessing

When is your next extended family meal? Consider printing out these words and singing them as a table grace.

An Empty Place

Lord, there will be an empty place
at the Christmas table.
And I'm not able to face it alone.
Please pass a second helping of Your grace.
I can't seem to get enough of it these days.
The lights on the tree are all a blur
as I look through swollen eyes.
The carols catch in my throat.
Wise men and shepherds, angels and stars,
Christmas cards, candles and gifts,
they all used to move me,
but this year I'm scarred
by wounds too fresh to heal.
I'm scared, too, by what I feel.
Haunting memories, good ones, but regrets too.
Too many tears. Too few Kleenex.
Too many days in December.
And all because the one I love is dead.
My heart feels dead as well.
I'm so afraid of what still lies ahead.
Please remind me that Easter
and all that it promises
will soon be here.
Maybe by then
I can celebrate the good tidings of Christmas
in spite of this empty chair.
In the name of Emmanuel I pray. Amen.

*Consider honoring that loved one who recently died by
setting a place for them at your family table.*

The Day Before Christmas

It's the day before Christmas
and your shopping's not done.
You've maxed out the VISA and Capital One.
Your kids are expecting a flat screen TV,
a Tivo, an X-box and even a Wii.
They have no idea how bad things have got
and how much your stomach's
all tied up in knots.
The market is iffy. Your job's insecure
and plans for next summer
have lost their allure.

The Spirit of Christmas seems way beyond reach
It's like you've been drained
by a joy-sucking leech.
In twenty-four hours the big day arrives,
and like old man Scrooge
your heart's shriveled in size.
But lest you give up and turn into the Grinch,
consider this game plan
to ease Humbug's pinch.

Just take time to chill out. Warm up by the fire.
Then prayerfully ponder your heartfelt desire.
To count all your blessings that money can't buy.
Like children who hug you and puppies that try.
The vows at your wedding.
Your mate's faithfulness.
Their mute understanding and tender caress.

A bank full of memories that no one can rob.
Your grandfather's watch
with his antique gold fob.
The wealth of true friendship.
A chum's knowing glance.
And when you have screwed up,
that prized second chance.
A healthy awareness of all you can do.
Those talents God gave you that help define you.

That fireside reflection
should brighten your mood.
By adding up blessings you start feeling good.
In spite of these hard times, recession and debt,
you're really quite wealthy. You tend to forget
that *Joy to the World* is much more than a song.
It's what you can give
even when you been wronged.

When you feel contented
without lusting for more,
you give from your heart
not some shelf at a store.
The best gifts you wrap aren't expensive you see.
Their priceless and costly and yet they are free.

That brings us to Christmas. That miracle birth.
A young virgin mother who doubted her worth.
The manger. The angels.
The shepherds who came.
A baby long-promised to free us from shame.

A human-wrapped present no one could afford
was offered without charge.
That babe was the Lord.
That's it in a nutshell. He's God's gift of love.
The Present (or Presence)
we all have dreamed of.
Amazingly awesome. Too good to be true.
Attempts to earn Heaven are over.
They're through.

So don't sweat tomorrow.
Just let Christmas come.
In light of its message, be grateful. Have fun.
Expect imperfection. Accept what you get.
Be thankful and patient. Let go of regrets.
Give grace when offended. Extend tenderness.
And when the day's over your soul will feel blest.

Read The Gospel According to John chapter 3, verses 16-17.

A Universal Cry for Joy

Anyone can understand
a baby's cry. In any land
a lexicon's not needed
for the language is the same.

And so it was when that one child
was born the night that Heaven smiled.
A baby cried and in that sound
the voice of God was heard.

In Holland, Haiti, Greece and Spain,
in Egypt, China and Bahrain
the Christmas message is the same.
In Christ God speaks His heart.

Ironically that baby's cry
from one whose mission was to die
was not a scream of grief or pain.
It was the cry of joy.

Joy to the World, all nations sing
and like the bells that chime and ring
this joyful message needs no words.
That universal cry conveys God's love.

*Why do you think Christmas continues to be such a
popular holiday in cultures where Christianity is not a
growing religion?*

'Twas the Day After Christmas

The families have gone.
The gifts put away.
One last look at the cards friends have sent.
I love the day after
to pause and reflect.
And as carols still play, I'm content.

It's a day to be quiet
and sit by the fire
while sifting through memories we've made.
I'm grateful for photographs
faded and torn
that capture the past on parade.

It's a day to be grateful
that Christmas extends
through the choices we make through the year.
The gift of our presence
with family and friends
is a treasure to those we hold dear.

What do you enjoy most about the Christmas season?
With that in mind, what are some ways you can keep
the spirit of Christmas alive all year long?

All I Want for Christmas

It's a season of joy
that my sorrow has found
as these silent nights trigger my grief.
A loved one has left us
since Christmas last year.
And my laughter is seldom and brief.

It's the month of December
with carols and cards,
but my heart is too broken to care.
I'm lonely and anxious.
It feels like I'm lost.
A heaviness hangs in the air.

Traditions that moved me
for much of my life
(and music of Christmases past)
are trying my patience
and testing my faith.
How I wish that this month would go fast.

O God, all I want
for Christ's birthday this year
is the gift of Your Presence and peace.
Please grant me the means
to embrace what I feel
'til the nightmares of sorrow will cease.

*This poem is dedicated to my friends who have lost
mates and parents this year and now face their first
Christmas without them.*

A New Year's Hymn

As this New Year breaks upon us,
we anticipate Your grace.
Fresh as dew with each new morning,
You are present in this place.
Distance us from shame that haunts us.
Draw us closer to Your heart.
Help us glimpse the dawn before us
with the joy of brand new starts.

As this New Year breaks upon us
we anticipate Your power
to sustain us in our living
day-by-day and hour-by-hour.
Lord, infuse us with Your Spirit.
Fill us with the faith to trust
when our doubts deter our progress.
When resolve all turns to dust.

As this New Year breaks upon us
we anticipate Your plans
rooted in a heart of mercy
we don't always understand.
Please protect us as we venture
into vistas yet unknown.
Guardian of our tomorrows,
guide us from Your sovereign throne.

tune: *Joyful, Joyful We Adore Thee*

A New Year Now Has Dawned

A New Year now has dawned
inviting us to dream
of unity the likes of which
we've never seen.
God, give us grace
to mend our ways
and turn away
from what we've been.

A New Year now has dawned
inviting us to do
those acts of love
we have put off
You've called us to.
God, give us grace
to start afresh and see each task
as serving You.

A New Year now has dawned
inviting us to dare
to be the hands
and feet of Jesus everywhere.
God, give us grace
that we might risk
and in our risking, really care.

A New Year now has dawned
inviting us to be
a church that models hope
in our community.
God, give us grace
to claim a future marked by love
and dignity.

tune: We Come O Christ to Thee

*What is on your "wish list" for the church you attend?
Go ahead and fill this page with words and phrases
that describe the kind of church you long for. If you feel
so inclined, share your list with your pastor or priest.*

Longing for the Good Old Days

The way it was is gone for good,
but it sure was good back then.
No wonder we are always quick
to ask *"Remember when?"*

We savored life. We thanked the Lord
even though those times were tough.
We didn't have what we have now,
but we sure did have enough.

We scrimped and saved to get ahead,
but we mostly stayed behind.
Still, neighbors knew when we had needs
and helped us in a bind.

The good old days found us in church.
We made sure that we were there.
We were one nation under God,
so we took time for prayer.

But now it seems we're backwards-prone.
We are wealthy, but we're poor.
We've little time for those we love,
while jobs we hate take more.

But since we can't rewind the tape
to those days of yesteryear,
let's make the most of time God gives
and cherish those we're near.

What about "the good old days" do you miss the most?
Is there something you could do to recapture the essence
of that value in your family unit?

A Virtuous God, Who Can Find?

A God with the heart of a virtuous mother
who can find?
Her children trust in her
so that they don't not fear what is to come
This mother-like God
will do them good and not evil
all the days of their lives.

Like merchant ships that never anchor,
this God provides for those she loves
bringing food from afar.
Though man cannot live by bread alone,
this loving parent provides necessary nourishment
to her household.

While it is night
and those she birthed are fast asleep,
Mother slowly girds her loins with strength
and remains at work
before anyone else awakens.
She plants what we harvest.
She perceives what is good.
Her candle of compassion never is extinguished.
She stretches out her hand to the needy.
She wraps her comforting arms
around the poor.

This God does not want us to be afraid.
And the reason is simple to see.
Mother God clothes us in the beautiful raiment of
her presence.

Strength and honor are her clothing.
She rejoices in the future she controls.
From her mouth proceed the words of Life.
The law of kindness leaps from her tongue.
She capably looks out

for the wellbeing of her family.
Her children rise up and call her blessed.

*What characteristics of God (as represented in the Bible)
resemble what you most appreciated about your
mother? Make your own list in the space below.*

And God Created Mothers

On the eighth day of creation,
once the Lord God had His rest,
He created what (in retrospect)
we'd call His very best.
This new species He named mothers.
Adam's better-half with child.
Grace incarnate, strong yet tender.
An oasis in the wild.

And the Lord equipped this species
with a sixth sense and a heart
that can break, but keep on loving,
when sweet kids became quite tart.

Mothers see both front and backwards.
They survive on little sleep.
And though life can hurt them deeply,
you will rarely see them weep.

They persist when feel like quitting.
They forgive before they're asked.
They deny themselves routinely
rarely sidelined by a task.

When the Lord created mothers,
it was hardly just a whim.
His main purpose was to emulate
the love we find in Him.

*Reflect on your relationship with your mom. How did
she influence your life? What do you wish had been
different?*

My Mother's Hands

My mother's hands are gnarled
and quite wrinkled.
The kiss of time has left its beauty marks.
Those slender fingers clutch
for more than mem'ries.
They reach in love to comfort hurting hearts.
My mother's hands upraised in praise to Jesus
call me to worship and to seek His face.

My mother's hands still fold
to ask God's blessing.
They grasp His hand and hold on for dear life.
Much like a toddler takes her daddy's fingers,
my mother clings to God with knuckles white.
My mother's hands recall her deep devotion
inviting me to serve the Lord she loves.

My mother's hands are strangers to an iPad.
But they make music when she's asked to play.
An old upright or baby grand piano
provide the keys on which her fingers pray.
My mother's hand can entertain her neighbors
while worshiping the One who owns her heart.

My mother's hands
will one day cease their motion.
Deprived of life, they'll lay unclenched and still.
They will remind me of her faithful service
responding to a call that she fulfilled.
My mother's hands will on that day direct me
to fix my gaze on my eternal home.

Remember, to Give Thanks

Gratitude is based on memory.
So remember, to give thanks.
Mother's wise advice we'd all do well to mind.
When reminded of our blessings,
we recall how blessed we are
and begin to seek what God intends we find.

So perhaps what Mother told us
is the key to giving thanks.
Don't we all recall the words she'd often say?
"Now remember to say thank you
for the things that you've received.
Being grateful is a debt you have to pay."

It's entirely possible to be grateful without saying thank
you. But that's entirely inappropriate. Before the week
is over, send a thank you note or email to someone who
has helped you recently.

That Certain Someone

There is a certain someone
I've longed for all my life.

Someone to watch me catch the ball.
Someone to help me when I fall.
Someone to say *"I know you tried."*
Someone to listen to my whys.
Someone to pay when I just can't.
Someone to see things from my slant.
Someone to hold me when I'm scared.
Someone to make sure I'm prepared.

Someone who loves me yet says *"no"*
and when I protest lets me go.
Someone who waits till I return
and then inquires *"Whaddya learn?"*
Someone who knows me totally
and overlooks the worst in me.
Someone who takes me at my word
and doesn't judge me as absurd.

Someone whose dealings are quite fair.
He arbitrates to clear the air.
Someone whose hugs aren't always earned.
He never hoards the things he's learned.
Someone whose friendship is for keeps.
He prays for me before he sleeps.
Someone whose patience won't run dry.
He aches with me each time I cry.

This certain someone has a name
and though he'll never dance with fame,
today I'm feeling mighty glad
that God gave me this one called Dad.

*This poem is dedicated to my father who died
on November 4, 2008. It was a red letter day when the
White House was promised to our first black President. I
wrote it shortly before my father's death.*

*In the space below write a letter to your dad. Even
though he may be deceased, express what you
appreciated about him and what you wish had been
different in your relationship. Be honest. Write with a
view of grace, forgiveness and humility.*

And God Created Grandparents

Grandparents are what God designed
to underscore His grace.
Their love is unconditional
as shown by their embrace.

Their hugs convey how much they care.
Their words describe their pride.
A grandma and a grandpa
make you feel so good inside.

Grandparents tend to bend the rules
and grant what you request.
They've learned that life says "no" too much
and so they're prone to "yes."

A grandma and a grandpa know
to give their brood a break
for looking back they both recall
how much their hearts would ache.

Grandparents are the means by which
the Lord helps children see
how faith that's tested through the years
withstands adversity.

They silently draw kids to Christ
without much need for words.
Their actions speak up for themselves
as what is lived is heard.

*What did you most appreciate about your
grandparents? Be as specific as you can.*

What Grandparents Dream for Grandkids

As you sleep I dream for you
a world where peace will reign
where cures for cancer will be found
and hope will conquer pain.

I'm trusting, much-loved little one,
that you will grow to find
a world where kings and presidents
are known for being kind.

I pray you'll be protected
from the evil in this world
and that you'll sense God's presence
as your future is unfurled.

But until then, my precious child,
relax and rest assured
that love will guide you every day.
For that you have my word.

List your grandchildren by name. Next to their name
write one word that celebrates something about them for
which you are grateful.

Now that I am Old and Gray

"Now that I am old and gray..."
I love to hear the psalmist say
those seven words that resonate
with people much like we.

He doesn't sugar-coat the facts.
We're shrinking much like melting wax.
Like candles that are burning down,
our wicks our flickering.

Our vision blurs. Our memories fail.
Like week-old bread, we're growing stale.
Our bodies ache. We're moving slow.
He's right. We're old and gray.

Our dreams of what we hoped to do
are still unmet. It's sad, but true.
Our bucket list has been replaced
by lots of pills to take.

There's less of life that looms ahead
than what we've lived. And soon we're dead.
And yet he says we have a task
that we'd best not ignore.

We've all been called to testify
while we've still time, before we die.
The witness stand awaits each one
to share what we've observed.

To validate that God is just.
To speak on His behalf. We must.
His reputation is at stake.
The courtroom is all ears.

And though, like Moses, words don't flow,
what matters most is what we know.
The things we've seen time and again
are written in our hearts.

How God came through when all seemed lost,
those times He proved that He was boss,
when sure defeat proved not to be
and in the end we won.

How faith survived when doubts assailed
or when the family business failed.
How starting over gave us pause
to learn from our mistakes.

How purposed generosity
was used by God to set us free
from greed and all it promised
when in truth it was a lie.

How death wreaked havoc in our home
and left us reeling all alone,
but how God came as Comforter
and healed our broken hearts.

And how unfounded nasty lies
kept us from gaining what we prize
and yet how God gave us the grace
to cope and to forgive.

Our children and grandchildren, too,
must hear from us before life's through.
The things we say might very well
help lead them to the Lord.

So even though you're old and gray,
don't think you haven't much to say.
The wealth of years is yours to spend.
It is your legacy.

This poem is based on Psalm 71.

*What if today were your last day of life? What would
you want your grandchildren to remember about you?
Use the space below to share your thoughts.*

When Someone You Love Has Dementia

When someone you love doesn't know it is you,
you die just a little unsure what to do.
But then as their eyes smile
and twinkle with joy,
you know that you still have a bond.

When someone you love
has been robbed of their mind,
they say things that hurt you.
They aren't always kind.
But then you remember their memory is shot
and actions are fueled by their fear.

When someone you love is confused and afraid,
you suffer in silence, but still wouldn't trade
the gift of their presence and all that they are
and who they have been through the years.

When someone you love
has forgotten your name,
you swallow your pride
and then make it your aim
to be fully present and reach for their hand
and gently remind them they're loved.

There are people in your life who struggled with memory issues that you will never forget. Who are they? Why do they continue to mean so much to you?

The Fruit of Love

The fruit of love, this gift of life,
we place, O God, within your care.
To know your grace and guiding hand
in years to come is now our prayer.

This tender child is known by You,
inclined to truth and evil too.
Would you protect this one we love
from sin and harm its whole life through?

A baby's future waits with hope
enveloped with the Spirit's grace.
Tomorrow's promise can be glimpsed
within this infant's tiny face.

With humble joy we recognize
a task that only has begun.
A sacred charge lies in our arms
to cradle faith and pass it on.

Whether your faith tradition practices infant baptism or infant dedication, this is a prayer that you can personalize. Who is that new addition to your extended family? Use the words of this poem as you pray for the child and the parents.

God Be Praised for Recreation

God, be praised for recreation
walking, running, sailing, too.
We love golf and tennis, don't we?
Flying kites in skies of blue.
Playing Bridge and taking photos
help us to relax and rest.
Recreation is required
if we hope to be our best.

God, be praised for His example
to unplug and call it quits.
Those who fail to keep a Sabbath,
risk the loss of health and wits.
Leisure is a sacred calling.
Rest is what our bodies need.
Balance is what God intended
for His creatures to succeed.

God, be praised for work and playtime.
Both are needed in our lives.
Honest labor gives us value.
Sports and hobbies help us thrive.
God who made us for His purpose
wired us to find the joys
that we knew at playground recess
as young girls and as young boys.

tune: Joyful, Joyful We Adore Thee

Have you ever noticed that the words re-creation and recreation are spelled the same? Reflect on how your favorite hobby can be a source of spiritual renewal.

Lord, We Are Grateful

Lord, we are grateful for those who love us;
those we call family, those who are friends.
Loved, we can face the pressures life sends us.
Through those we cherish, Your love descends.

Lord, we are grateful for Your creation;
trees in fall splendor, dark stormy skies.
Nature reminds us of Your strong power.
Majestic beauty dazzles ours eyes.

Lord, we are grateful for Your rich mercy,
fresh as the morning, new every day.
Sin is forgiven. Guilt has been buried.
Gone is the debt we never could pay.

tune: Morning Has Broken

*Have you ever tried writing an original hymn? The tune
for "Morning Has Broken" is a very sing-able melody.
Why not try your hand at writing a verse that celebrates
that for which you are grateful? Start with "Lord, we are
grateful...." and see where it goes.*

Depression's Pall

The music of my soul has ceased
and all because a heartless beast
refuses to release its grip
and set my spirit free.

The big black dog. A dark gray cloud.
Depression's pall is like a shroud
that wraps around my lifeless soul
and robs my joy of air.

Depression is a living death
depriving me of needed breath.
It mocks my faith incessantly
while holding hostage hope.

O Giver of eternal light
illuminate this endless night
and lead me from this prison cell
into the warmth of day.

Winston Churchill struggled with depression. He's the one who called it "the black dog." What other words or phrases could be used to describe this "dark night of the soul?"

A Family Reunion Prayer

Creator of our family tree
(especially the branch called "me")
please let our roots grow deep and strong
so it will stand secure.

From limb to limb our tree has grown.
And, Lord, You've seen how winds have blown.
But, by Your grace strong storms could not
uproot what You preserve.

Allow the blossoms on our tree
to scent our world most fragrantly.
And may the fruit that we will bear
help nourish those You love.

Within the shadow of our tree,
may friends and strangers come to see
the love that binds each one of us
in spite of miles and years.

*In the space below you can sketch your own family tree.
You don't have to be an artist. Start underground with
the roots of grandparents and parents. The trunk of the
tree is you. The branches that grow from the trunk are
your children and grandchildren. Have fun!*

God Remains Our Source of Courage

God remains our source of courage
when we're traumatized by terror.
When we're haunted by the headlines
and the heartache everywhere.
Hear God whisper in the silence,
"Don't despair, I'm in control.
Hurting hearts and broken cities
will at last one day be whole."

God invites us to be trusting
when we find that faith is hard.
When we're fearful for our safety
and our nerves are frayed or jarred.
Still God whispers in the silence,
"Even when your faith is weak,
I will keep your feet from stumbling
when your way is dark and bleak."

What national news finds you "haunted by the
headlines?" List the recent current events to which this
prayer would apply.

A Milestone Birthday

This week I reached that storied age
where (as I reach to turn the page)
I realize my book called LIFE
is racing toward the end.

At sixty-five I don't feel old.
But (based on what I have been told)
there are some folks who just might choose
to celebrate with me.

Arthur Rightus is a pain.
When he shows up, he leaves me lame.
And where Art goes, Ben Gay is sure to
tag along as well.

Dee Mentia can be such a jerk.
She shows up at my place of work
and steals all kinds of memories.
I think that Dee is cruel.

Ty Lenol and Anna Sen
have been my parents' trusted friends.
But these two chums can wait their turn.
Right now, I'm feeling fine.

And then there's Cole Lenoscopy.
He's quite invasive, don't you see?
I cringe whenever Cole's around.
He leaves me awfully drained.

Jerry Attricks thinks it's time
I join him for a glass of whine.
But I'm not ready to admit
his club is where I fit.

So much for folks who want to be
invited to my grand party.
I think a dinner with my wife
is all I really want.

*Even though this poem pokes fun of growing older,
aches and pains associated with age aren't a laughing
matter. Reflect on how the increasing number of candles
on your birthday cake coincides with the number of
challenges you have to face each year. Who do you have
to talk to about the challenges of aging?*

I Will Praise the Lord

I will praise the Lord who stands beside me
when my life is hanging by a thread.
Since His plans for me cannot be thwarted,
I won't worry but rejoice instead.
I will praise the Lord though crisis finds me,
for I know His everlasting arms
will embrace me so as to protect me
when I'm traumatized by sudden harm.

I will praise the Lord who knows my future
whose design incorporates my past.
Though I've questioned
how the Lord could use me,
He reminds me I still have a task.
I will praise the Lord who reigns in Heaven
for I know He has complete control
of what happens to my life and through me.
I am His, my body, mind and soul.

I will praise the Lord who knows my weakness
whose great mercy overcomes my fear.
When I fail to trust what He has promised,
grace reminds me He is always here.
I will praise the Lord of second chances
for I know He will not let me go.
He will guide me on my faith-filled journey
even though my progress may be slow.

tune: Day by Day and with Each Passing Moment

*Read the words of Saint Paul as recorded in The Epistle
to the Romans chapter 8, verses 18-39.*

Spring Trumpets a Theological Truth

The blossoms on our cherry tree
bear witness to the fact
that Old Man Winter's death
has been confirmed.
The rumors of his final days
proved more than gossiping.
Just ask the robin pulling at a worm.

Yes, winter's given way to spring
(and just in time me thinks).
The toll the snow and cold took was intense.
The endless weeks of winter's woes
found joy in short supply.
Those nonstop sunless days
would make me wince.

But now a smile frames my face.
There's evidence of life
as light and color warm my thawing bones.
The truth of Easter's not reserved
for just one holy day.
Spring trumpets...
"Death is trumped by Christ alone."

*Have you ever contemplated the theological implications
of winter transitioning to spring? What is it about
springtime that results in a spring to your step? To what
do you most look forward each spring?*

Easter Jazz

A blue note heard on Friday
had been coaxed from sorrow's horn.
Clarinets, trumpets and saxes
moaned in time 'til Sunday morn.

And then (oh my) such music!
With the sunrise (saints alive!)
there were flutes, French horns and cellos
making melodies that jived.

Add some trombones. Cue the tubas,
violins, guitars and drums.
There was all that jazz (and then some)
praising God for Kingdom come.

Women mourning started dancing
to the herd of thundering notes
as the Prince of Joy (now risen)
donned His resurrection coat.

O my Lord, it was some morning.
Bourbon Street could ne'er compare
to the music born that Easter
and the song that filled the air.

The theme of resurrection and music tend to go together.
What music do you tend to associate with Easter?

Creation Hymn

Azure skies, magenta sunsets,
emerald forests, turquoise seas,
golden deserts, clear blue rivers,
charcoal mountains, autumn trees.
These are colors of God's pallet
from which come a masterpiece.
Beauty crowns creations glory.
Natures wonders never cease.

Waterfalls and windswept canyons,
flowering meadows, gurgling brooks,
crashing waves and melting glaciers
steal our breath with every look.
All creation is a portrait
of the Artist's grand design
framed with love for our enjoyment
hung upon the wall of time.

Awed by what we see around us,
we declare God's Majesty.
All that dwells within the atom.
Microscopic symmetry.
Mathematic calculations.
Telescopic views of space.
In creation God reveals
His nature to the human race.

tune: Joyful, Joyful We Adore Thee

Hawaiian 23rd Psalm

The Lord is my oarsman.
He steers my canoe
and paddles me safely to shore.
He whispers aloha
and calls me by name
while pointing to what lies in store.

The palm trees that sway
and the tropical breezes
portray what awaits when I die.
Such beauty, refreshment,
contentment and peace.
And pleasure that money can't buy.

And though I may falter,
and fall on my face,
the Lord walks with me in the sand.
His goodness surrounds me
and steadies my step.
His mercy will help me to stand.

He bids me draw close,
drapes a lei round my neck
and tells me I've nothing to fear.
"I'll never forsake you.
I'll always provide
and I promise I'll always be near."

Why not try your own hand at paraphrasing the 23rd
Psalm? Start by finding words that express God's
promised provision in your life.

There's Aloha All Around Us

I bring God's sweet aloha
when I come to work each day.
I convey this message
by the shirts I wear.
Though the sunshine may be missing,
the sweet warmth of God abounds
in each face that we encounter everywhere.

There's aloha in the rhodies,
in the dahlias or a rose.
There's aloha in the dogwood trees and grass.
You can sense God's awesome presence
in the eagles overhead
or a bench named for a loved one
who has passed.

There's aloha in a sunrise
that illuminates the lake
or in a summer storm that lights the sky.
There's aloha in a cookout
with a group of caring friends.
It's a peace and joy that money cannot buy!

Since aloha means *"good morning,"*
"you are welcome" or *"be blessed,"*
I'm inclined to wear a shirt that says it all.
Paradise is all around us
if we take the time to see
or to listen to a seagull's evening call.

*This poem is dedicated to the residents of Covenant
Living at the Shores where I serve as chaplain*

God's Aloha

I offer God's aloha.
It's a way to say you're loved.
It's a one-word blessing people long to hear.
Aloha is a greeting
that means so much more than hi.
It's a reassurance that our God is near.

I give you God's aloha.
It's a tender sweet goodbye.
As you leave please know that you are not alone.
Aloha means God's with you
and the trade winds of His grace
will both warm and guide you
as you journey on.

Create an acronym for ALOHA. (For example, Amazing Love Overshadows Helpless Adventurers)

Diversity University

Diversity University
is a process not a place.
It's the school that we attend our whole life long.
It's the classroom where we must unlearn
the lies that we were taught
when as children we accepted what was wrong.

Diversity University
helps us read another's eyes
and then study what is written on their face.
It's where we confront our bias
and do homework on our own
as we reflect on God's amazing grace.

Diversity University
is the means by which we grow
to become the persons God meant us to be.
It's where we accept our classmates
as deserving to be loved
while we celebrate the right to disagree.

Diversity University
is challenging for sure.
It's the hardest 'college' anyone attends.
To make the grade we swallow pride
and sip humility.
It's a learning process that just never ends.

Make a list in your head or on paper of people groups to which you have trouble relating or accepting. Ask God to help you have an open heart and mind.

The Olympics of Daily Life

The Olympics of life are a constant affair.
There's the balance beam of work and play.
There's wrestling worries and hurdling fear
while pole vaulting problems each day.

There's swimming upstream
'gainst the current of wrong.
There's diving into what needs done.
There's dashing from breakfast
to rush-hour grid.
It's a race meant for rats that we run.

There's the relay of faith
where we pass the baton
to both children and grandkids alike.
Yes, we need to be fit
as we all exercise
trusting Jesus with all of our might.

So, Lord, won't you coach us
to do what it takes
to finish while doing our best?
Please give us endurance
for what comes our way
and then help us to face every test.

What event in Olympics of Daily Life comes most easy to you? Which one is most difficult?

Our Father in Heaven

Our Father in Heaven, we pause now to pray
while enveloped by pressures on earth.
We struggle to trust You when life hems us in
or when critics may question our worth.

We honor Your name: Elohim, Adonai,
El Shaddai, Tzevaot, Yahweh, too.
Most Holy, Almighty, Compassionate One,
You are just, ever faithful and true.

We welcome Your Kingdom,
Your Highness, we're Yours,
surrendered to what You allow.
Your will is what matters
for You know what's best.
So we (in humility) bow.

May You reign supremely in Heaven and here
accomplishing what You deem best.
A Kingdom of kindness, forgiveness and love,
of order, rich beauty, and rest.

We pray that this day
we'll be nourished with food,
by our friendships, the arts, and Your Word.
Our bodies and spirits rely on Your grace
lest our focus on Truth becomes blurred.

Forgive us our failures, O Father, we pray.
We stumble so often it seems.
Our willful desires breed actions that wound
while exposing our self-centered schemes.

But only forgive us, dear Father, we pray
as we are inclined to forgive
the ones who have wronged us.
May we offer grace
even though it's so hard to give.

Temptations that threaten our lives loom ahead.
Like landmines they can't be perceived.
Please, Father, protect us
and guard us from harm
and the evil that seeks to deceive.

Deliver us daily from sin's unseen traps
that trip up those blind to their pride.
Admitting our weakness, we ask for Your help,
God of mercy in You we confide.

For Yours is the Kingdom to which we belong.
It's glory, dominion and might
defy understanding and can't be explained
by the smartest (no matter how bright).

By faith we submit to Your unending reign.
As Your children we live quite assured
that what You intend, loving Father, is good.
And that what we've just prayed
has been heard. Amen!

*In what way does this paraphrase of the Lord's Prayer
help you understand Jesus' original prayer?*

Pour Your Spirit on Your Church

Pour Your Spirit on Your people.
Fill Your Church, O God, we pray.
Help us navigate the culture
lest (confused) we lose our way.
Guide us with a holy passion
to pursue Your righteousness.
Keep us focused on Your precepts
grounded in Your holiness.

Help Your people love like Jesus.
Motivate us to be kind
as we stand for timeless virtues
lost amid the daily grind.
Teach us Christlike perseverance
as we earn the right to speak
to the ones You long to pardon.
Make us merciful and meek.

Breathe, O breathe, Your breath upon us.
Animate our focused will.
Fuel our mission to be mindful
of Your Word that guides us still.
Keep us anchored in Your Scriptures.
Hold our feet to purging fire
so to help us stand unflinching
known by love and Your desire.

tune: Joyful, Joyful We Adore Thee

A May Prayer

May you discover in this month
that Easter's not a day,
but rather it's a way of life
by which faith learns to play!

May you experience the joy
just knowing Jesus lives!
May you not fear what's still to come
but trust a God who gives.

May you determine to give thanks
for all that's going right.
May you look past another's wrong
so you'll sleep well at night.

May you dust for God's fingerprints
in all that springtime brings:
a flow'ring shrub, a fragrant rose,
the tune a songbird sings.

May you decide to make a friend
of someone you don't know.
May you mend frayed relationships
although you cannot sew.

May you delight in getting fit
by walking every day.
May you eat what is good for you
and chart how much you weigh.

May you take time to talk to God
and then to contemplate
the ways the Lord has answered prayer
with *"Yes"* and *"No"* and *"Wait!"*

May you begin each day this month
by reading from God's Word
and listening expectantly
for what the ancients heard.

May you unwrap each day as if
the present is a gift.
And may God's presence grant you peace
and give your soul a lift.

*Write your own May prayer in the space below.
Compose a letter to your Heavenly Father expressing
the desires of your heart. Be honest. Be specific.
Conclude your letter with these words... "May it come to
be, dear Lord, I pray. Amen."*

Spiritual Wellness

I've come to see that wellness
is much more than being fit.
A healthy body needs a healthy soul.
While dieting and exercise can do a body good,
a person really needs a higher goal.

It's great to run a marathon
or jog five times a week,
but running after peace has merit, too.
And while walking before supper
can burn dreaded calories,
a daily walk with God is good for you.

To bend and flex has merit.
So, we strive to stay in shape.
As we age we must maintain agility.
But God also wants to stretch us
to expand our usefulness.
It's His will that we become all we can be.

Yes, our bodies are a temple
that deserve refurbishment
lest through disrepair they start to fall apart.
But a temple's just a building
if it's just an empty shell.
So let's exercise our souls and guard our hearts.

*Time for a check-up. Would you say you are more fit
physically or spiritually? How can you improve in both
areas?*

I Prayed for You Today

Even though I wasn't sure
exactly what to say,
I talked to God and spoke your name.
I prayed for you today.

I asked the Lord to give you strength
to calm you from your stress,
to free you from the things you fear
and bathe your mind with rest.

I asked the Lord to help you
in the uphill days to come;
I asked our precious loving God
to complete what He's begun.

He whispered in the quiet
and filled my heart with peace.
He said that you are deeply loved
and that His love won't cease.

*As you might notice, this was printed earlier in the book
as a "Dear George Letter." This prayer is one you can
copy and send to someone going through a hard time.*

A One Word Prayer

I just breathe the name of Jesus
when my heart is filled with fear.
And though I cannot see His face,
I know that He is near.

When I whisper "Jesus" softly
I'm admitting I'm in need.
By calling out that precious name,
my stress-bound soul is freed.

It's a one-word prayer I utter
when I'm not sure what to pray.
It's a prayer of sweet surrender
when I'm weary of "my way."

I pray "Jesus" when I'm worried
or when I am depressed.
I say "Jesus" when my mind's confused
or when my life's a mess.

It's a prayer He always answers
as He gives me eyes to see
evidences of His presence
and His tender love for me.

Songwriter Bill Gaither wrote the Gospel hymn "There's Something About That Name." What is it about Jesus' name that comforts and consoles? Try creating an acronym for JESUS. (For example, Justice Expressed, Salvation Unveiled, Satisfaction)

Life is Like a Cup of Tea

Life is like a cup of tea,
at least that's how it seems to me.
It's bold and sweet and tastes the best
when sipped with those you love.

It has to steep to turn out great.
But life, like tea, is worth the wait.
Though, if we're honest, we'd admit
delays are sometimes hard.

Like fragile China porcelain,
our bodies, marred and chipped by sin,
are delicate and prone to crack.
Eventually they break!

But when our lives at last are through,
the grace of God (like Super Glue)
will mend the shards that were our cups
and fill us with new life.

It's all because of Calvary,
where Innocence poured out like tea
emptied Himself of Heaven's Blend
and drank what we deserved.

*What current circumstances in your life are causing you
to "steep?" Ask God for the patience to wait out the
"brewing process."*

The Gospel According to Baseball

It's a game that's based on bases,
first and second, third and home.
And the rules remain consistent
whether played in Rome or Nome.

You must first head straight to first base.
You can't skip it or take third.
Without rules there'd be no meaning.
Without rules games are absurd.

And the game of life's no different.
Those who play it on their own
think that they can skip the bases
and then slide in late at home.

But there's order to the process.
We must take each stage in stride.
Someone pitches us the Gospel
and explains why Jesus died.

First, we must accept forgiveness
that He gave us on the cross.
After that, it's on to second
where we let Him be the boss.

Then we're third-base-bound by serving
those around us who have needs.
And it's likely we'll remain there
'til we've lost our pride and greed.

Then, in time, our Coach will motion
that it's time to head for home.
That's the time we'll claim our vict'ry
as the King smiles from His throne.

So the moral of this poem
is to let the game you love
help you understand the ground rules
that apply to what's above.

*Baseball has four bases that must be touched in order.
Have you ever heard of the Four Spiritual Laws? Why
not Google them to learn more?*

The Gospel According to Eight Ball

Within the middle of the rack
there is one special ball
that has a certain power all its own.
But, if pocketed too early,
there's a penalty to pay.
It's the ball by which
this billiard game is known.

The eight ball is "the Lord of all"
deserving of respect.
Unlike the stripes and solids, it is king.
By virtue of its right to reign,
this ball dictates the rules.
And those who follow them have right to sing.

The one who wins at last confronts
the eight ball with the cue
and makes the orb of black his finally aim.
By honoring its presence,
what is last gives way to first.
Without that ball you cannot win the game.

In life, Christ is the eight ball.
He's unique, unlike the rest.
When we disregard His right to rule, we lose.
But by honoring His order,
we can make the Lord our aim.
That encounter is our purpose. It's Good News!

*Who do you know who enjoys playing billiards? Rack
you brain and then consider sending this poem to them.*

Caring for One Another

As Christians we're a family.
That means that I'm your brother.
It also means we have a job
to care for one another.

A family does not ignore
the needs of dad or mother.
The siblings know their first concern
is loving one another.

And even when it takes some time
and feels like it's a bother,
inconvenience is the price
of serving one another.

We are not meant to be alone.
God gave us one another.
That's why we grieve when someone leaves
'cause we need one another.

Grief robs our joy and steals our peace.
It's unlike any other.
So, you need me and I need you
to comfort one another.

Did you know there are 59 "one another" statements in the New Testament? That's an indication how important "family" is to our Heavenly Father. How can "community" become more meaningful to you?

Oh, The Places You Will Go
A graduation poem with apologies to Dr. Seuss

The world's your oyster. The world's your stage.
Your time has come. You've reached the age.
The Lord will guide you. So, trust his plans.
Just say, *"Your wish is my command."*

Look in your heart. What brings delight?
Embrace your gift. Turn on the light.
God made you just the way you are.
So go with that and you'll go far.

But far begins with one small step.
So lace your shoes and then expect
to run your race at your own speed.
Don't fret about who's in the lead.

This thing called life's a marathon.
It's not a sprint. So, carry on!
Along the way, you'll trip and fall.
You'll bruise your knees and that's not all.

Your pride will smart, but that's okay.
That's how you learn to make your way.
So, each new day look in the mirror.
Confront yourself and what you fear.

Look deep inside at what you see.
Reflect on who you long to be.
Don't overlook what you don't like.
Tell bents you hate to take a hike.

Be honest with the one you face
embracing God's amazing grace.
It covers all you dare confess
and undermines perfection's stress.

Be sure to give yourself a smile.
It's good to celebrate each mile.
Along the path that you will go,
who cares if you go fast or slow?

The speed that marks your upward climb
means not so much so never mind.
The trek you take is most unique.
So, too, the plans you aim to seek.

Dream big. Imagine. Go for broke.
While some may laugh, it is no joke.
Remind yourself God's in control
and He will help you reach your goals.

You will achieve more than you know.
The many places you will go
cannot be seen from where you sit.
You have to move out bit by bit.

Make every day your chance to start
to live your dream and own your part
in what the good Lord longs to bless
including you and your success.

What matters most is making time
to pace yourself and read the signs
of where to go and what to do.
The future does depend on you.

This poem is dedicated to my nephew William Cameron Romig in celebration of his graduation from high school.

Who do you know who is about to graduate from high school or college? This poem might inspire you to write your own poem to celebrate their achievements.

Life is Precious

Life is precious, sacred, blest
from the womb to final rest.
God is in a child's first breath
or a grandpa facing death.

Special-needs autistic son.
Crippled daughter who can't run.
Those impaired in speech or sight.
Those whose hearing isn't right.

Those who can't recall their name.
Those with damage to their brain.
Those in prison, addicts too.
Those who think their options few.

Each life matters. Each has worth.
Everyone on "God's green earth."
Life is precious, sacred, blest
from the womb to final rest.

Read Psalm 139. What new insights come to mind about the sanctity of life? Is it comforting or concerning that you are not hidden from God no matter where you are?

The Waiting Room

The waiting room is a lonely place
where I must face
my grownup childhood fears.
Surrounded by others,
I feel alone and nervous
about what's to come.
It's a gathering place
for family and friends
where memories are shared
and regrets embraced.
It's where goodbyes are said
to someone who cannot return the farewell.

It's a sacred place
where earth and heaven meet.
As faith and hope hold hands,
mortality gives way to immortality.
It's where the mystery of eternal light
provides illumination amid the shadows
to approach God with confidence.
It's holy ground.

The waiting room provides a front row seat
as the drama of life and death is played out
on the elevated stage of a hospice bed
while a loved one takes one last curtain call.
The waiting room is a difficult place to be.
But there is no place I would rather be.
It is an awesome privilege to shepherd this one
who escorted me into this world into the next.

Lord, give me grace for the journey ahead
and the means to cherish
each remaining moment with my mom.

*The poem was written as I observed my 92 year old
mother living out the final days of her life after suffering
a major stroke and being put on hospice.*

*Reflect on the correlations between a waiting room in a
hospital and the waiting room of Eternity. What comes
to mind you've never considered before?*

So Blessed Are We

So long ago God whispered in a garden,
it is not good for us to be alone.
We need companionship and affirmation
Life can be hard, our hearts as hard as stone.
We long to be both understood and valued
encouraged in the gifts by which we're known.

So steep, so difficult, the trail we're climbing.
At times we wonder if we can go on.
We slip and fall. And often we are bleeding.
Our journey can seem tortuous and long.
But when we walk in step with one another,
the darkest night becomes a hopeful dawn.

So let us be transparent with each other
confessing things we hope for, fear and need.
Without the insight that a friend can offer,
we're often blind to ego, lust and greed.
Temptation's hold on us is strangely weakened
when linked in prayer, we boldly intercede.

So blessed are we to be joined to each other
on this adventure that we share as one.
The curse of loneliness has now been broken,
The joy of Heaven seems to have begun.
What God intended for His chosen offspring,
we know firsthand through friendship with His Son.

tune: Be Still, my Soul, the Lord is on Thy Side

Epiloque:

A Book Called "Myself"

So, what then will be your life story?
It's a book that you're writing each day.
You're unique, so I guess it's a novel.
Still, your future's a big mystery.

Your story is bound to be noticed
by those who observe what you write.
Will your words offer Christ-like compassion
with phrases of reasoned insight?

Will your sentences question the culture
as you challenge the lies it conveys?
Will your paragraphs stand out in bold print
as you stand up to ungodly ways?

Will your story be read by the masses?
Or will it be left on some shelf?
The things that you write
on each day's empty page
will result in a book called *"Myself."*

*If you think of your life as a book, what chapter titles
would you give to what you've lived thus far? What
chapter title would you choose to summarize how you
want your life to end?*

About the Author

The Reverend Greg Asimakoupoulos has been called America's pastor/poet laureate. Over the past forty years he has served congregations in California, Illinois and Washington. He has written over two hundred magazine articles and a dozen books including "Finding God in It's a Wonderful Life."

Pastor Greg currently writes a faith and values column for three newspapers. His weekly internet blog is entitled "Rhymes and Reasons" and can be accessed at www.partialobserver.com

Hiligaynon Language:
101 Hiligaynon Verbs

BY ANJ SANTOS

Contents

1. To accept: baton   1

2. To admit: aku   2

3. To answer: sabat   3

4. To appear: pakita   4

5. To ask: pamangkot   5

6. To be: mangin, nangin   6

7. To be able to: maka, naka   7

8. To become: mangin, nangin   8

9. To begin: sugod   9

10. To break: buka   10

11. To breath: ginhawa   11

12. To buy: bakal   12

13. To call: tawag   13

14. To can: sarang   14

15. To choose: pili   15

16. To close: sira   17

17. To come: abot   18

18. To cook: luto   19

19. To cry: hibi   20

20. To dance: saot   21

21. To decide: desisyon   22

22. To decrease: buhin   23

23. To die: patay, tagumatayon   24

24. To do: himo   25

25. To drink: inom   26

26. To drive : maneho   27

27. To eat: kaon   28

28. To enter: sulod   29

29. To exit: gua   30

30. To explain: paathag   31

31. To fall: hulog, kahulog   32

32. To feel: batyag   33

33. To fight: away   34

34. To find: kita, pangita   35

35. To finish: tapos   36

36. To fly: lupad   37

37. To forget: kalimtan   38

38. To get up: bangon   39

39. To give: hatag   40

40. To go: kadto   41

41. To happen: tabo, katabo   42

42. To have: na, naga   43

43. To hear: bati, batian, pamatian   44

44. To help: bulig, buligan   45

45. To hold: uyat, uyatan   47

46. To increase: dugang   48

47. To introduce: pakilala   49

48. To invite: agda   50

49. To kill: patay   51

50. To kiss: halok, halukan   52

51. To know: hibalo, hibaluan   53

52. To laugh: kadlaw   54

53. To learn: tuon   55

54. To lie down: higda   56

55. To like: gustuhan   57

56. To listen: pamati   58

57. To live: kabuhi   59

58. To lose: dula   60

59. To love: higugma, higugmaon   61

60. To meet: sugata   62

61. To need: kinahanglan   63

62. To notice: talupangdan, talupangod, talupangdon   64

63. To open: buksan   66

64. To play: hampang   67

65. To put: butang   68

66. To read: basa   70

67. To receive: baton   71

68. To remember: dumdom   72

69. To repeat: sulit   74

70. To return: balik   75

71. To run: dalagan   76

72. To say: siling   78

73. To scream: singgit   79

74. To see: kita   80

75. To seem: daw   81

76. To sell: baligya   82

77. To send: padala   83

78. To show: pakita   84

79. To sing: kanta   86

80. To sit down: pungko   87

81. To sleep: tulog   88

82. To smile: yuhom   89

83. To speak: hambal   90

84. To stand: tindog   91

85. To start: sugod   92

86. To stay: istar   93

87. To take: kuha   94

88. To talk: istorya   96

89. To teach: tudlo   97

90. To think: hunahuna   98

91. To touch: tandog   100

92. To travel: byahe   102

93. To understand: hangop, hangpan   103

94. To use: gamit   104

95. To wait: hulat   105

96. To walk: lakat   106

97. To want: gusto, gustuhan   107

98. To watch: tan-aw   108

99. To win: daog   109

100. To work: obra   110

101. To write: sulat   111

1. To accept: baton

Tenses	Word	Examples
Past Simple	_**Gin**_baton	_Ginbaton_ niya ang obra. (He _accepted_ the work.)
Past Continuous	_**Gin**_baton	_Ginbaton_ niya ang obra. (He _was accepting_ the work.)
Past Perfect Simple	_**Gin**_baton _**na**_	_Ginbaton na_ niya ang obra. (He _had accepted_ the work.)
Past Perfect Continuous	_**Gin**_baton _**pa**_	_Ginbaton pa_ niya ang obra. (He _had been accepting_ the work.)
Present Simple	_**Gina**_baton	_Ginabaton_ niya ang obra. (He _accepts_ the work.)
Present Continuous	_**Gina**_baton	_Ginabaton_ niya ang obra. (He _is accepting_ the work.)
Present Perfect Simple	_**Gina**_baton _**na**_	_Ginabaton na_ niya ang obra. (He _has accepted_ the work.)
Present Perfect Continuous	_**Gina**_baton _**pa**_	_Ginabaton pa_ niya ang obra. (He _has been accepting_ the work.)
Future Simple	_**Maga**_baton	_Magabaton_ sia sang obra. (He _will accept_ the work.)
Future Continuous	_**Maga**_baton	_Magabaton_ sia sang obra. (He _will be accepting_ the work.)
Future Perfect Simple	_**Maga**_baton _**na**_	_Magabaton na_ kuntani sia sang obra. (He _will have accepted_ the work by then.)
Future Perfect Continuous	_**Maga**_baton _**pa**_	_Magabaton pa_ sia sang obra. (He _will have been accepting_ the work.)

2. To admit: aku

Tenses	Word	Examples
Past Simple	**Nag**-aku	*Nag-aku* sia sang iya sala. (He *admitted* his sin.)
Past Continuous	**Nag**-aku	*Nag-aku* sia sang iya sala. (He *was admitting* his sin.)
Past Perfect Simple	**Gin**-aku **na**	*Gin-aku na* niya ang iya sala. (He *had admitted* his sin.)
Past Perfect Continuous	**Gin**-aku **pa**	*Gin-aku pa* niya ang iya sala. (He *had been admitting* his sin.)
Present Simple	**Naga**aku	*Nagaaku* sia sang iya sala. (He *admits* his sin.)
Present Continuous	**Naga**aku	*Nagaaku* sia sang iya sala. (He *is admitting* his sin.)
Present Perfect Simple	**Gina**aku **na**	*Ginaaku na* niya ang iya sala. (He *has admitted* his sin.)
Present Perfect Continuous	**Gina**aku **pa**	*Ginaaku pa* niya ang iya sala. (He *has been admitting* his sin.)
Future Simple	**Maga**aku	*Magaaku* sia sang iya sala. (He *will admit* his sin.)
Future Continuous	**Maga**aku	*Magaaku* sia sang iya sala. (He *will be admitting* his sin.)
Future Perfect Simple	**Maga**aku **na**	*Magaaku na* kuntani sia sang iya sala. (He *will have admitted* his sin by then.)
Future Perfect Continuous	**Maga**aku **pa**	*Magaaku pa* sia sang iya sala. (He *will have been admitting* his sin.)

2

3. To answer: sabat

Tenses	Word	Examples
Past Simple	*Gin*sabat	*Ginsabat* niya ang telepono. (He *answered* the telephone.)
Past Continuous	*Gin*sabat	*Ginsabat* niya ang telepono. (He *was answering* the telephone.)
Past Perfect Simple	*Gin*sabat **na**	*Ginsabat na* niya ang telepono. (He *had answered* the telephone.)
Past Perfect Continuous	*Gin*sabat **pa**	*Ginsabat pa* niya ang telepono. (He *had been answering* the telephone.)
Present Simple	*Gina*sabat	*Ginasabat* niya ang telepono. (He *answers* the telephone.)
Present Continuous	*Gina*sabat	*Ginasabat* niya ang telepono. (He *is answering* the telephone.)
Present Perfect Simple	*Gina*sabat **na**	*Ginasabat na* niya ang iya sala. (He *has answered* the telephone.)
Present Perfect Continuous	*Gina*sabat **pa**	*Ginasaba pa* niya ang telepono. (He *has been answering* the telephone.)
Future Simple	*Maga*sabat	*Magasabat* sia sang telepono. (He *will answer* the telephone.)
Future Continuous	*Maga*sabat	*Magasabat* sia sang telepono. (He *will be answering* the telephone.)
Future Perfect Simple	*Maga*sabat **na**	*Magasabat na* kuntani sia sang telepono. (He *will have answered* the telephone by then.)
Future Perfect Continuous	*Maga*sabat **pa**	*Magasabat pa* sia sang telepono. (He *will have been answering* the telephone.)

4. To appear: pakita

Tenses	Word	Examples
Past Simple	*Nag*pakita	*Nagpakita* sia sa korte. (He *appeared* to the court.)
Past Continuous	*Nag*pakita	*Nagpakita* sia sa korte. (He *was appearing* to the court.)
Past Perfect Simple	*Nag*pakita *na*	*Nagpakita na* sia sa korte. (He *had appeared* to the court.)
Past Perfect Continuous	*Nag*pakita *pa*	*Nagpakita pa* sia sa korte. (He *had been appearing* to the court.)
Present Simple	*Naga*pakita	*Nagapakita* sia sa korte. (He *appears* to the court.)
Present Continuous	*Naga*pakita	*Nagapakita* sia sa korte. (He *is appearing* to the court.)
Present Perfect Simple	*Naga*pakita *na*	*Nagapakita na* sia sa korte. (He *has appeared* to the court.)
Present Perfect Continuous	*Naga*pakita *pa*	*Nagapakita pa* sia sa korte. (He *has been appearing* to the court.)
Future Simple	*Maga*pakita	*Magapakita* sia sa korte. (He *will appear* to the court.)
Future Continuous	*Maga*pakita	*Magapakita* sia sa korte. (He *will be appearing* to the court.)
Future Perfect Simple	*Maga*pakita *na*	*Magapakita na* kuntani sia sa korte. (He *will have appeared* to the court by then.)
Future Perfect Continuous	*Maga*pakita *pa*	*Magapakita pa* sia sa korte. (He *will have been appearing* to the court.)

4

5. To ask: pamangkot

Tenses	Word	Examples
Past Simple	**Nag**pamangkot	*Nagpamangkot* sia sa iya iloy. (He *asked* his mother.)
Past Continuous	**Nag**pamangkot	*Nagpamangkot* sia sa iya iloy. (He *was asking* his mother.)
Past Perfect Simple	**Nag**pamangkot **na**	*Nagpamangkot na* sia sa iya iloy. (He *had asked* his mother.)
Past Perfect Continuous	**Naga**pamangkot **pa**	*Nagapamangkot pa* sia sa iya iloy. (He *had been asking* his mother.)
Present Simple	**Naga**pamangkot	*Nagapamangkot* sia sa iya iloy. (He *asks* his mother.)
Present Continuous	**Naga**pamangkot	*Nagapamangkot* sia sa iya iloy. (He *is asking* his mother.)
Present Perfect Simple	**Naga**pamangkot **na**	*Nagapamangkot na* sia sa iya iloy. (He *has asked* his mother.)
Present Perfect Continuous	**Naga**pamangkot **pa**	*Nagapamangkot pa* sia sa iya iloy. (He *has been asking* his mother.)
Future Simple	**Maga**pamangkot	*Magapamangkot* sia sa iya iloy. (He *will ask* his mother.)
Future Continuous	**Maga**pamangkot	*Magapamangkot* sia sa iya iloy. (He *will be asking* his mother.)
Future Perfect Simple	**Maga**pamangkot **na**	*Magapamangkot na* kuntani sia sa iya iloy. (He *will have asked* his mother by then.)
Future Perfect Continuous	**Maga**pamangkot **pa**	*Magapamangkot pa* sia sa iya iloy. (He *will have been asking* his mother.)

6. To be: mangin, nangin

Tenses	Word	Examples
Past Simple	No equivalent	No equivalent
Past Continuous	No equivalent	No equivalent
Past Perfect Simple	*Nangin*	*Nangin* mabuot sia nga bata. (He *had been* a good child.)
Past Perfect Continuous	No equivalent	No equivalent
Present Simple	*Mangin*	*Mangin* mabuot nga bata. (*Be* a good child.)
Present Continuous	No equivalent	No equivalent
Present Perfect Simple	*Nangin*	*Nangin* mabuot sia nga bata. (He *has been* a good child.)
Present Perfect Continuous	No equivalent	No equivalent
Future Simple	No equivalent	No equivalent
Future Continuous	No equivalent	No equivalent
Future Perfect Simple	No equivalent	No equivalent
Future Perfect Continuous	No equivalent	No equivalent

7. To be able to: maka, naka

Tenses	Word	Examples
Past Simple	No equivalent	No equivalent
Past Continuous	*Naka*	*Nakabisita* sia sa akon kahapon. (He _was able_ to visit me yesterday.)
Past Perfect Simple	No equivalent	No equivalent
Past Perfect Continuous	*Naka*	*Nakabisita na* sia sa akon kahapon. (He _had been able_ to visit me yesterday.)
Present Simple	No equivalent	No equivalent
Present Continuous	No equivalent	No equivalent
Present Perfect Simple	No equivalent	No equivalent
Present Perfect Continuous	No equivalent	No equivalent
Future Simple	No equivalent	No equivalent
Future Continuous	*Maka*	*Maka*bisita sia sa akon buas. (He _will be able to_ visit me tomorrow.)
Future Perfect Simple	No equivalent	No equivalent
Future Perfect Continuous	No equivalent	No equivalent

8. To become: mangin, nangin

Tenses	Word	Examples
Past Simple	*Nangin*	*Nangin* mapagros sia. (He *became* healthy.)
Past Continuous	*Nangin*	*Nangin* mapagros sia. (He *was becoming* healthy.)
Past Perfect Simple	*Nangin*	*Nangin* mapagros sia. (He *had became* healthy.)
Past Perfect Continuous	*Nangin*	*Nangin* mapagros sia. (He *had been becoming* healthy.)
Present Simple	*Mangin*	*Mangin* mapagros sia. (He *becomes* healthy.)
Present Continuous	*Mangin*	*Mangin* mapagros sia. (He *is becoming* healthy.)
Present Perfect Simple	*Nangin*	*Nangin* mapagros sia. (He *has become* healthy.)
Present Perfect Continuous	*Nangin*	*Nangin* mapagros sia. (He *has been becoming* healthy.)
Future Simple	*Mangin*	*Mangin* mapagros sia. (He *will be* healthy.)
Future Continuous	*Mangin*	*Mangin* mapagros sia. (He *will be becoming* healthy.)
Future Perfect Simple	*Mangin*	*Mangin* mapagros sia kuntani. (He *will have become* healthy by then.)
Future Perfect Continuous	*Mangin*	*Mangin* mapagros sia. (He *will have been becoming* healthy.)

9. To begin: sugod

Tenses	Word	Examples
Past Simple	*Nag*sugod	*Nagsugod* sia sa paglibot. (He *began* to move around.)
Past Continuous	*Nag*sugod	*Nagsugod* sia sa paglibot. (He *was beginning* to move around.)
Past Perfect Simple	*Nag*sugod *na*	*Nagsugod na* sia sa paglibot. (He *had began* to move around.)
Past Perfect Continuous	*Nag*sugod *pa*	*Nagsugod pa* sia sa paglibot. (He *had been beginning* to move around.)
Present Simple	*Naga*sugod	*Nagasugod* sia sa paglibot. (He *begins* to move around.)
Present Continuous	*Naga*sugod	*Nagasugod* sia sa paglibot. (He *is beginning* to move around.)
Present Perfect Simple	*Naga*sugod *na*	*Nagasugod na* sia sa paglibot. (He *has began* to move around.)
Present Perfect Continuous	*Naga*sugod *pa*	*Nagasugod pa* sia sa paglibot. (He *has been beginning* to move around.)
Future Simple	*Maga*sugod	*Magasugod* sia sa paglibot. (He *will begin* to move around.)
Future Continuous	*Maga*sugod	*Magasugod* sia sa paglibot. (He *will be beginning* to move around.)
Future Perfect Simple	*Maga*sugod *na*	*Magasugod na* kuntani sia sa paglibot. (He *will have begun* to move around by then.)
Future Perfect Continuous	*Maga*sugod *pa*	*Magasugod pa* sia sa paglibot. (He *will have been beginning* to move around.)

10. To break: buka

Tenses	Word	Examples
Past Simple	**Gin**buka	*Ginbuka* niya ang bintana. (He *broke* the window.)
Past Continuous	**Gin**buka	*Ginbuka* niya ang bintana. (He *was breaking* the window.)
Past Perfect Simple	**Gin**buka **na**	*Ginbuka na* niya ang bintana. (He *had broken* the window.)
Past Perfect Continuous	**Gin**buka **pa**	*Ginbuka pa* niya ang bintana. (He *had been breaking* the window.)
Present Simple	**Gina**buka	*Ginabuka* niya ang bintana. (He *breaks* the window.)
Present Continuous	**Gina**buka	*Ginabuka* niya ang bintana. (He *is breaking* the window.)
Present Perfect Simple	**Gina**buka **na**	*Ginabuka na* niya ang bintana. (He *has broken* the window.)
Present Perfect Continuous	**Gina**buka **pa**	*Ginabuka pa* niya ang bintana. (He *has been breaking* the window.)
Future Simple	**Paga**buk-on	*Pagabuk-on* niya ang bintana. (He *will break* the window.)
Future Continuous	**Paga**buk-on	*Pagabuk-on* niya ang bintana. (He *will be breaking* the window.)
Future Perfect Simple	**Paga**buk-on **na**	*Pagabuk-on na* kuntani niya ang bintana. (He *will have broken* the window by then.)
Future Perfect Continuous	**Paga**buk-on **pa**	*Pagabuk-on pa* niya ang bintana. (He *will have been breaking* the window.)

11. To breath: ginhawa

Tenses	Word	Examples
Past Simple	*Nag*ginhawa	*Nagginhawa* sia. (He *breathed*.)
Past Continuous	*Nag*ginhawa	*Nagginhawa* sia. (He *was breathing*.)
Past Perfect Simple	*Nag*ginhawa *na*	*Nagginhawa na* sia. (He *had breathed*.)
Past Perfect Continuous	*Nag*ginhawa *pa*	*Nagginhawa pa* sia. (He *had been breathing*.)
Present Simple	*Naga*ginhawa	*Nagaginhawa* sia. (He *breaths*.)
Present Continuous	*Naga*ginhawa	*Nagaginhawa* sia. (He *is breathing*.)
Present Perfect Simple	*Naga*ginhawa *na*	*Nagaginhawa na* sia. (He *has breathed*.)
Present Perfect Continuous	*Naga*ginhawa *pa*	*Nagaginhawa pa* sia. (He *has been breathing*.)
Future Simple	*Maga*ginhawa	*Magaginhawa* sia. (He *will breath*.)
Future Continuous	*Maga*ginhawa	*Magaginhawa* sia. (He *will be breathing*.)
Future Perfect Simple	*Maga*ginhawa *na*	*Magaginhawa na* sia kuntani. (He *will have breathed* by then.)
Future Perfect Continuous	*Maga*ginhawa *pa*	*Magaginhawa pa* sia. (He *will have been breathing*.)

12. To buy: bakal

Tenses	Word	Examples
Past Simple	*Nag*bakal	*Nagbakal* sila sang ila pagkaon. (They *bought* their food.)
Past Continuous	*Nag*bakal	*Nagbakal* sila sang ila pagkaon. (They *were buying* their food.)
Past Perfect Simple	*Nag*bakal *na*	*Nagbakal na* sila sang ila pagkaon. (They *had bought* their food.)
Past Perfect Continuous	*Nag*bakal *pa*	*Nagbakal pa* sila sang ila pagkaon. (They *had been buying* their food.)
Present Simple	*Naga*bakal	*Nagabakal* sila sang ila pagkaon. (They *buy* their food.)
Present Continuous	*Naga*bakal	*Nagabakal* sila sang ila pagkaon. (They *are buying* their food.)
Present Perfect Simple	*Naga*bakal *na*	*Nagabakal na* sila sang ila pagkaon. (They *have bought* their food.)
Present Perfect Continuous	*Naga*bakal *pa*	*Nagabakal pa* sila sang ila pagkaon. (They *have been buying* their food.)
Future Simple	*Maga*bakal	*Magabakal* sila sang ila pagkaon. (They *will buy* their food.)
Future Continuous	*Maga*bakal	*Magabakal* sila sang ila pagkaon. (They *will be buying* their food.)
Future Perfect Simple	*Maga*bakal *na*	*Magabakal na* kuntani sila sang ila pagkaon. (They *will have bought* their food by then.)
Future Perfect Continuous	*Maga*bakal *pa*	*Magabakal pa* sila sang ila pagkaon. (They *will have been buying* their food.)

13. To call: tawag

Tenses	Word	Examples
Past Simple	**Nag**tawag	*Nagtawag* sia sa telepono. (He *called* in the telephone.)
Past Continuous	**Nag**tawag	*Nagtawag* sia sa telepono. (He *was calling* in the telephone.)
Past Perfect Simple	**Nag**tawag **na**	*Nagtawag na* sia sa telepono. (He *had called* in the telephone.)
Past Perfect Continuous	**Nag**tawag **pa**	*Nagtawag pa* sia sa telepono. (He *had been calling* in the telephone.)
Present Simple	**Naga**tawag	*Nagatawag* sia sa telepono. (He *calls* in the telephone.)
Present Continuous	**Naga**tawag	*Nagatawag* sia sa telepono. (He *is calling* in the telephone.)
Present Perfect Simple	**Naga**tawag **na**	*Nagatawag na* sia sa telepono. (He *has called* in the telephone.)
Present Perfect Continuous	**Naga**tawag **pa**	*Nagatawag pa* sia sa telepono. (He *has been calling* in the telephone.)
Future Simple	**Maga**tawag	*Magatawag* sia sa telepono. (He *will call* in the telephone.)
Future Continuous	**Maga**tawag	*Magatawag* sia sa telepono. (He *will be calling* in the telephone.)
Future Perfect Simple	**Maga**tawag **na**	*Magatawag na* kuntani sia sa telepono. (He *will have called* in the telephone by then.)
Future Perfect Continuous	**Maga**tawag **pa**	*Magatawag pa* sia sa telepono. (He *will have been calling* in the telephone.)

14. To can: sarang

Tenses	Word	Examples
Past Simple	**_Naka_**sarang	_Nakasarang_ ako sang obra. (I _could_ do the work.)
Past Continuous	No equivalent	No equivalent
Past Perfect Simple	No equivalent	No equivalent
Past Perfect Continuous	No equivalent	No equivalent
Present Simple	**_Maka_**sarang	_Makasarang_ ako sang obra. (I _can_ do the work.)
Present Continuous	No equivalent	No equivalent
Present Perfect Simple	No equivalent	No equivalent
Present Perfect Continuous	No equivalent	No equivalent
Future Simple	No equivalent	No equivalent
Future Continuous	No equivalent	No equivalent
Future Perfect Simple	No equivalent	No equivalent
Future Perfect Continuous	No equivalent	No equivalent

15. To choose: pili

Tenses	Word	Examples
Past Simple	**Nag**pili	*Nagpili* ako sang maayo nga mga kaupdanan. (I *chose* my associates wisely.)
Past Continuous	**Nag**pili	*Nagpili* ako sang maayo nga mga kaupdanan. (I *was choosing* my associates wisely.)
Past Perfect Simple	**Nag**pili *na*	*Nagpili na* ako sang maayo nga mga kaupdanan. (I *had chosen* my associates wisely.)
Past Perfect Continuous	**Nag**pili *pa*	*Nagpili pa* ako sang maayo nga mga kaupdanan. (I *had been choosing* my associates wisely.)
Present Simple	**Naga**pili	*Nagapili* ako sang maayo nga mga kaupdanan. (I *choose* my associates wisely.)
Present Continuous	**Naga**pili	*Nagapili* ako sang maayo nga mga kaupdanan. (I *am choosing* my associates wisely.)
Present Perfect Simple	**Naga**pili *na*	*Nagapili na* ako sang maayo nga mga kaupdanan. (I *have chosen* my associates wisely.)
Present Perfect Continuous	**Naga**pili *pa*	*Nagapili pa* ako sang maayo nga mga kaupdanan. (I *have been choosing* my associates wisely.)
Future Simple	**Maga**pili	*Magapili* ako sang maayo nga mga kaupdanan. (I *will choose* my associates wisely.)
Future Continuous	**Maga**pili	*Magapili* ako sang maayo nga mga kaupdanan. (I *will be choosing* my associates wisely.)

Future Perfect Simple	_**Maga**pili_ _**na**_	_Magapili na_ kuntani ako sang maayo nga mga kaupdanan. (I _will have chosen_ my associates wisely by then.)
Future Perfect Continuous	_**Maga**pili_ _**pa**_	_Magapili pa_ ako sang maayo nga mga kaupdanan. (I _will have been choosing_ my associates wisely.)

16. To close: sira

Tenses	Word	Examples
Past Simple	*Gin*sira	*Ginsira* ni Ana ang bintana. (Ana *closed* the window.)
Past Continuous	*Gin*sira	*Ginsira* ni Ana ang bintana. (Ana *was closing* the window.)
Past Perfect Simple	*Gin*sira *na*	*Ginsira na* ni Ana ang bintana. (Ana *had closed* the window.)
Past Perfect Continuous	*Gin*sira *pa*	*Ginsira pa* ni Ana ang bintana. (Ana *had been closing* the window.)
Present Simple	*Gina*sira	*Ginasira* ni Ana ang bintana. (Ana *closes* the window.)
Present Continuous	*Gina*sira	*Ginasira* ni Ana ang bintana. (Ana *is closing* the window.)
Present Perfect Simple	*Gina*sira *na*	*Ginasira na* ni Ana ang bintana. (Ana *has closed* the window.)
Present Perfect Continuous	*Gina*sira *pa*	*Ginasira pa* ni Ana ang bintana. (Ana *has been closing* the window.)
Future Simple	*Maga*sira	*Magasira* si Ana sang bintana. (Ana *will close* the window.)
Future Continuous	*Maga*sira	*Magasira* si Ana sang bintana. (Ana *will be closing* the window.)
Future Perfect Simple	*Maga*sira *na*	*Magasira na* kuntani si Ana sang bintana. (Ana *will have closed* the window by then.)
Future Perfect Continuous	*Maga*sira *pa*	*Magasira pa* si Ana sang bintana. (Ana *will have been closing* the window.)

17. To come: abot

Tenses	Word	Examples
Past Simple	_Nag_-abot	_Nag-abot_ sila sa husto nga oras. (They _came_ at the right time.)
Past Continuous	_Nag_-abot	_Nag-abot_ sila sa husto nga oras. (They _were coming_ at the right time.)
Past Perfect Simple	_Nag_-abot _na_	_Nag-abot na_ sila sa husto nga oras. (They _had came_ at the right time.)
Past Perfect Continuous	_Nag_-abot _pa_	_Nag-abot pa_ sila sa husto nga oras. (They _had been coming_ at the right time.)
Present Simple	_Naga_abot	_Nagaabot_ sila sa husto nga oras. (They _come_ at the right time.)
Present Continuous	_Naga_abot	_Nagaabot_ sila sa husto nga oras. (They _are coming_ at the right time.)
Present Perfect Simple	_Naga_abot _na_	_Nagaabot na_ sila sa husto nga oras. (They _have come_ at the right time.)
Present Perfect Continuous	_Naga_abot _pa_	_Nagaabot pa_ sila sa husto nga oras. (They _have been coming_ at the right time.)
Future Simple	_Maga_abot	_Magaabot_ sila sa husto nga oras. (They _will come_ at the right time.)
Future Continuous	_Maga_abot	_Magaabot_ sila sa husto nga oras. (They _will be coming_ at the right time.)
Future Perfect Simple	_Maga_abot _na_	_Magaabot na_ kuntani sila sa husto nga oras. (They _will have come_ at the right time by then.)
Future Perfect Continuous	_Maga_abot _pa_	_Magaabot pa_ sila sa husto nga oras. (They _will have been coming_ at the right time.)

18. To cook: luto

Tenses	Word	Examples
Past Simple	*Nag*luto	*Nagluto* si Nanay sang amon pagkaon. (Mother *cooked* our food.)
Past Continuous	*Nag*luto	*Nagluto* si Nanay sang amon pagkaon. (Mother *was cooking* our food.)
Past Perfect Simple	*Nag*luto *na*	*Nagluto na* si Nanay sang amon pagkaon. (Mother *had cooked* our food.)
Past Perfect Continuous	*Nag*luto *pa*	*Nagluto pa* si Nanay sang amon pagkaon. (Mother *had been cooking* our food.)
Present Simple	*Naga*luto	*Nagaluto* si Nanay sang amon pagkaon. (Mother *cooks* our food.)
Present Continuous	*Naga*luto	*Nagaluto* si Nanay sang amon pagkaon. (Mother *is cooking* our food.)
Present Perfect Simple	*Naga*luto *na*	*Nagaluto na* si Nanay sang amon pagkaon. (Mother *has cooked* our food.)
Present Perfect Continuous	*Naga*luto *pa*	*Nagaluto pa* si Nanay sang amon pagkaon. (Mother *has been cooking* our food.)
Future Simple	*Maga*luto	*Magaluto* si Nanay sang amon pagkaon. (Mother *will cook* our food.)
Future Continuous	*Maga*luto	*Magaluto* si Nanay sang amon pagkaon. (Mother *will be cooking* our food.)
Future Perfect Simple	*Maga*luto *na*	*Magaluto na* kuntani si Nanay sang amon pagkaon. (Mother *will have cooked* our food by then.)
Future Perfect Continuous	*Maga*luto *pa*	*Magaluto pa* si Nanay sang amon pagkaon. (Mother *will have been cooking* our food.)

19. To cry: hibi

Tenses	Word	Examples
Past Simple	**Nag**hibi	*Naghibi* ang lapsag. (The baby *cried*.)
Past Continuous	**Nag**hibi	*Naghibi* ang lapsag. (The baby *was crying*.)
Past Perfect Simple	**Nag**hibi ***na***	*Naghibi na* ang lapsag. (The baby *had cried*.)
Past Perfect Continuous	**Nag**hibi ***pa***	*Naghibi pa* ang lapsag. (The baby *had been crying*.)
Present Simple	**Naga**hibi	*Nagahibi* ang lapsag. (The baby *cries*.)
Present Continuous	**Naga**hibi	*Nagahibi* ang lapsag. (The baby *is crying*.)
Present Perfect Simple	**Naga**hibi ***na***	*Nagahibi na* ang lapsag. (The baby *has cried*.)
Present Perfect Continuous	**Naga**hibi ***pa***	*Nagahibi pa* ang lapsag. (The baby *has been crying*.)
Future Simple	**Maga**hibi	*Magahibi* ang lapsag. (The baby *will cry*.)
Future Continuous	**Maga**hibi	*Magahibi* ang lapsag. (The baby *will be crying*.)
Future Perfect Simple	**Maga**hibi ***na***	*Magahibi na* kuntani ang lapsag. (The baby *will have cried* by then.)
Future Perfect Continuous	**Maga**hibi ***pa***	*Magahibi pa* ang lapsag. (The baby *will have been crying*.)

20

20. To dance: saot

Tenses	Word	Examples
Past Simple	**Nag**saot	*Nagsaot* sila sang chacha. (They *danced* chacha.)
Past Continuous	**Nag**saot	*Nagsaot* sila sang chacha. (They *were dancing* chacha.)
Past Perfect Simple	**Nag**saot **na**	*Nagsaot na* sila sang chacha. (They *had danced* chacha.)
Past Perfect Continuous	**Nag**saot **pa**	*Nagsaot pa* sila sang chacha. (They *had been dancing* chacha.)
Present Simple	**Naga**saot	*Nagasaot* sila sang chacha. (They *dance* chacha.)
Present Continuous	**Naga**saot	*Nagasaot* sila sang chacha. (They *are dancing* chacha.)
Present Perfect Simple	**Naga**saot **na**	*Nagasaot na* sila sang chacha. (They *have danced* chacha.)
Present Perfect Continuous	**Naga**saot **pa**	*Nagasaot pa* sila sang chacha. (They *have been dancing* chacha.)
Future Simple	**Maga**saot	*Magasaot* sila sang chacha. (They *will dance* chacha.)
Future Continuous	**Maga**saot	*Magasaot* sila sang chacha. (They *will be dancing* chacha.)
Future Perfect Simple	**Maga**saot **na**	*Magasaot na* kuntani sila sang chacha. (They *will have danced* chacha by then.)
Future Perfect Continuous	**Maga**saot **pa**	*Magasaot pa* sila sang chacha. (They *will have been dancing* chacha.)

21. To decide: desisyon

Tenses	Word	Examples
Past Simple	**Nag**desisyon	*Nagdesisyon* sia para sa pamilya. (He *decided* for the family.)
Past Continuous	**Nag**desisyon	*Nagdesisyon* sia para sa pamilya. (He *was deciding* for the family.)
Past Perfect Simple	**Nag**desisyon **na**	*Nagdesisyon na* sia para sa pamilya. (He *had decided* for the family.)
Past Perfect Continuous	**Nag**desisyon **pa**	*Nagdesisyon pa* sia para sa pamilya. (He *had been deciding* for the family.)
Present Simple	**Naga**desisyon	*Nagadesisyon* sia para sa pamilya. (He *decides* for the family.)
Present Continuous	**Naga**desisyon	*Nagadesisyon* sia para sa pamilya. (He *is deciding* for the family.)
Present Perfect Simple	**Naga**desisyon **na**	*Nagadesisyon na* sia para sa pamilya. (He *has decided* for the family.)
Present Perfect Continuous	**Naga**desisyon **pa**	*Nagadesisyon pa* sia para sa pamilya. (He *has been deciding* for the family.)
Future Simple	**Maga**desisyon	*Magadesisyon* sia para sa pamilya. (He *will decide* for the family.)
Future Continuous	**Maga**desisyon	*Magadesisyon* sia para sa pamilya. (He *will be deciding* for the family.)
Future Perfect Simple	**Maga**desisyon **na**	*Magadesisyon na* kuntani sia para sa pamilya. (He *will have decided* for the family by then.)
Future Perfect Continuous	**Maga**desisyon **pa**	*Magadesisyon pa* sia para sa pamilya. (He *will have been deciding* for the family.)

22. To decrease: buhin

Tenses	Word	Examples
Past Simple	*Nag*buhin	*Nagbuhin* sila sang ila empleyado. (They *decreased* their employees.)
Past Continuous	*Nag*buhin	*Nagbuhin* sila sang ila empleyado. (They *were decreasing* their employees.)
Past Perfect Simple	*Nag*buhin *na*	*Nagbuhin na* sila sang ila empleyado. (They *had decreased* their employees.)
Past Perfect Continuous	*Nag*buhin *pa*	*Nagbuhin pa* sila sang ila empleyado. (They *had been decreasing* their employees.)
Present Simple	*Naga*buhin	*Nagabuhin* sila sang ila empleyado. (They *decrease* their employees.)
Present Continuous	*Naga*buhin	*Nagabuhin* sila sang ila empleyado. (They *are decreasing* their employees.)
Present Perfect Simple	*Naga*buhin *na*	*Nagabuhin na* sila sang ila empleyado. (They *have decreased* their employees.)
Present Perfect Continuous	*Naga*buhin *pa*	*Nagabuhin pa* sila sang ila empleyado. (They *have been decreasing* their employees.)
Future Simple	*Maga*buhin	*Magabuhin* sila sang ila empleyado. (They *will decrease* their employees.)
Future Continuous	*Maga*buhin	*Magabuhin* sila sang ila empleyado. (They *will be decreasing* their employees.)
Future Perfect Simple	*Maga*buhin *na*	*Magabuhin na* kuntani sila sang ila empleyado. (They *will have decreased* their employees by then.)
Future Perfect Continuous	*Maga*buhin *pa*	*Magabuhin pa* sila sang ila empleyado. (They *will have been decreasing* their employees.)

23. To die: patay, tagumatayon

Tenses	Word	Examples
Past Simple	_Na_patay	_Napatay_ sia bangod sang kanser. (He _died_ because of cancer.)
Past Continuous	_Na_patay	_Napatay_ sia bangod sang kanser. (He _was dying_ because of cancer.)
Past Perfect Simple	_Na_patay **_na_**	_Napatay na_ sia bangod sang kanser. (He _had died_ because of cancer.)
Past Perfect Continuous	_Nag_tagumatayon **_pa_**	_Nagtagumatayon pa_ sia bangod sang kanser. (He _had been dying_ because of cancer.)
Present Simple	_Na_patay	_Napatay_ sia bangod sang kanser. (He _dies_ because of cancer.)
Present Continuous	_Naga_tagumatayon	_Nagatagumatayon_ sia bangod sang kanser. (He _is dying_ because of cancer.)
Present Perfect Simple	_Na_patay **_na_**	_Napatay na_ sia bangod sang kanser. (He _has died_ because of cancer.)
Present Perfect Continuous	_Naga_tagumatayon **_pa_**	_Nagatagumatayon pa_ sia bangod sang kanser. (He _has been dying_ because of cancer.)
Future Simple	_Ma_patay	_Mapatay_ sia bangod sang kanser. (He _will die_ because of canser.)
Future Continuous	_Ma_patay	_Mapatay_ sia bangod sang kanser. (He _will be dying_ because of cancer.)
Future Perfect Simple	_Ma_patay **_na_**	_Mapatay na_ kuntani sia bangod sang kanser. (He _will have died_ because of cancer by then.)
Future Perfect Continuous	_Ma_patay **_pa_**	_Mapatay pa_ sia bangod sang kanser. (He _will have been dying_ because of cancer.)

24. To do: himo

Tenses	Word	Examples
Past Simple	*Nag*himo	*Naghimo* sila sang ila asaynment. (They *did* their assignment.)
Past Continuous	*Nag*himo	*Naghimo* sila sang ila asaynment. (They *were doing* their assignment.)
Past Perfect Simple	*Nag*himo *na*	*Naghimo na* sila sang ila asaynment. (They *had done* their assignment.)
Past Perfect Continuous	*Nag*himo *pa*	*Naghimo pa* sila sang ila asaynment. (They *had been doing* their assignment.)
Present Simple	*Naga*himo	*Nagahimo* sila sang ila asaynment. (They *do* their assignment.)
Present Continuous	*Naga*himo	*Nagahimo* sila sang ila asaynment. (They *are doing* their assignment.)
Present Perfect Simple	*Naga*himo *na*	*Nagahimo na* sila sang ila asaynment. (They *have done* their assignment.)
Present Perfect Continuous	*Naga*himo *pa*	*Nagahimo pa* sila sang ila asaynment. (They *have been doing* their assignment.)
Future Simple	*Maga*himo	*Magahimo* sila sang ila asaynment. (They *will do* their assignment.)
Future Continuous	*Maga*himo	*Magahimo* sila sang iia asaynment. (They *will be doing* their assignment.)
Future Perfect Simple	*Maga*himo *na*	*Magahimo na* kuntani sila sang ila asaynment. (They *will have done* their assignment by then.)
Future Perfect Continuous	*Maga*himo *pa*	*Magahimo pa* sila sang ila asaynment. (They *will have been doing* their assignment.)

25. To drink: inom

Tenses	Word	Examples
Past Simple	**_Nag_**-inom	_Nag-inom_ sia sang alak. (He _drank_ wine.)
Past Continuous	**_Nag_**-inom	_Nag-inom_ sia sang alak. (He _was drinking_ wine.)
Past Perfect Simple	**_Nag_**-inom **_na_**	_Nag-inom na_ sia sang alak. (He _had drank_ wine.)
Past Perfect Continuous	**_Nag_**-inom **_pa_**	_Nag-inom pa_ sia sang alak. (He _had been drinking_ wine.)
Present Simple	**_Naga_**inom	_Nagainom_ sia sang alak. (He _drinks_ wine.)
Present Continuous	**_Naga_**inom	_Nagainom_ sia sang alak. (He _is drinking_ wine.)
Present Perfect Simple	**_Naga_**inom **_na_**	_Nagainom na_ sia sang alak. (He _has drank_ wine.)
Present Perfect Continuous	**_Naga_**inom **_pa_**	_Nagainom pa_ sia sang alak. (He _has been drinking_ wine.)
Future Simple	**_Maga_**inom	_Magainom_ sia sang alak. (He _will drink_ wine.)
Future Continuous	**_Maga_**inom	_Magainom_ sia sang alak. (He _will be drinking_ wine.)
Future Perfect Simple	**_Maga_**inom **_na_**	_Magainom na_ kuntani sia sang alak. (He _will have drank_ wine by then.)
Future Perfect Continuous	**_Maga_**inom **_pa_**	_Magainom pa_ sia sang alak. (He _will have been drinking_ wine.)

26. To drive : maneho

Tenses	Word	Examples
Past Simple	*Nag*maneho	*Nagmaneho* sia sang kotse. (He *drove* the car.)
Past Continuous	*Nag*maneho	*Nagmaneho* sia sang kotse. (He *was driving* the car.)
Past Perfect Simple	*Nag*maneho *na*	*Nagmaneho na* sia sang kotse. (He *had drove* the car.)
Past Perfect Continuous	*Nag*maneho *pa*	*Nagmaneho pa* sia sang kotse. (He *had been driving* the car.)
Present Simple	*Naga*maneho	*Nagamaneho* sia sang kotse. (He *drives* the car.)
Present Continuous	*Naga*maneho	*Nagamaneho* sia sang kotse. (He *is driving* the car.)
Present Perfect Simple	*Naga*maneho *na*	*Nagamaneho na* sia sang kotse. (He *has drove* the car.)
Present Perfect Continuous	*Naga*maneho *pa*	*Nagamaneho pa* sia sang kotse. (He *has been driving* the car.)
Future Simple	*Maga*maneho	*Magamaneho* sia sang kotse. (He *will drive* the car.)
Future Continuous	*Maga*maneho	*Magamaneho* sia sang kotse. (He *will be driving* the car.)
Future Perfect Simple	*Maga*maneho *na*	*Magamaneho na* kuntani sia sang kotse. (He *will have driven* the car by then.)
Future Perfect Continuous	*Maga*maneho *pa*	*Magamaneho pa* sia sang kotse. (He *will have been driving* the car.)

27

27. To eat: kaon

Tenses	Word	Examples
Past Simple	**Nag**kaon	*Nagkaon* ako sang utan. (I *ate* vegetable.)
Past Continuous	**Nag**kaon	*Nagkaon* ako sang utan. (I *was eating* vegetable.)
Past Perfect Simple	**Nag**kaon **na**	*Nagkaon na* ako sang utan. (I *had eaten* vegetable.)
Past Perfect Continuous	**Nag**kaon **pa**	*Nagkaon pa* ako sang utan. (I *had been eating* vegetable.)
Present Simple	**Naga**kaon	*Nagakaon* ako sang utan. (I *eat* vegetable.)
Present Continuous	**Naga**kaon	*Nagakaon* ako sang utan. (I *am eating* vegetable.)
Present Perfect Simple	**Naga**kaon **na**	*Nagakaon na* ako sang utan. (I *have eaten* vegetable.)
Present Perfect Continuous	**Naga**kaon **pa**	*Nagakaon pa* ako sang utan. (I *have been eating* vegetable.)
Future Simple	**Maga**kaon	*Magakaon* ako sang utan. (I *will eat* vegetable.)
Future Continuous	**Maga**kaon	*Magakaon* ako sang utan. (I *will be eating* vegetable.)
Future Perfect Simple	**Maga**kaon **na**	*Magakaon na* kuntani ako sang utan. (I *will have eaten* vegetable by then.)
Future Perfect Continuous	**Maga**kaon **pa**	*Magakaon pa* ako sang utan. (I *will have been eating* vegetable.)

28. To enter: sulod

Tenses	Word	Examples
Past Simple	*Nag*sulod	*Nagsulod* sila sa kueba. (They *entered* in the cave.)
Past Continuous	*Nag*sulod	*Nagsulod* sila sa kueba. (They *were entering* in the cave.)
Past Perfect Simple	*Nag*sulod *na*	*Nagsulod na* sila sa kueba. (They *had entered* in the cave.)
Past Perfect Continuous	*Nag*sulod *pa*	*Nagsulod pa* sila sa kueba. (They *had been entering* in the cave.)
Present Simple	*Naga*sulod	*Nagasulod* sila sa kueba. (They *enter* in the cave.)
Present Continuous	*Naga*sulod	*Nagasulod* sila sa kueba. (They *are entering* in the cave.)
Present Perfect Simple	*Naga*sulod *na*	*Nagasulod na* sila sa kueba. (They *have entered* in the cave.)
Present Perfect Continuous	*Naga*sulod *pa*	*Nagasulod pa* sila sa kueba. (They *have been entering* in the cave.)
Future Simple	*Maga*sulod	*Magasulod* sila sa kueba. (They *will enter* in the cave.)
Future Continuous	*Maga*sulod	*Magasulod* sila sa kueba. (They *will be entering* in the cave.)
Future Perfect Simple	*Maga*sulod *na*	*Magasulod na* kuntani sila sa kueba. (They *will have entered* in the cave by then.)
Future Perfect Continuous	*Maga*sulod *pa*	*Magasulod pa* sila sa kueba. (They *will have been entering* in the cave.)

29. To exit: gua

Tenses	Word	Examples
Past Simple	*Nag*gua	*Naggua* sia sa sina nga puertahan. (He *exited* in that door.)
Past Continuous	*Nag*gua	*Naggua* sia sa sina nga puertahan. (He *was exiting* in that door.)
Past Perfect Simple	*Nag*gua *na*	*Naggua na* sia sa sina nga puertahan. (He *had exited* in that door.)
Past Perfect Continuous	*Nag*gua *pa*	*Naggua pa* sia sa sina nga puertahan. (He *had been exiting* in that door.)
Present Simple	*Naga*gua	*Nagagua* sia sa sina nga puertahan. (He *exits* in that door.)
Present Continuous	*Naga*gua	*Nagagua* sia sa sina nga puertahan. (He *is exiting* in that door.)
Present Perfect Simple	*Naga*gua *na*	*Nagagua na* sia sa sina nga puertahan. (He *has exited* in that door.)
Present Perfect Continuous	*Naga*gua *pa*	*Nagagua pa* sia sa sina nga puertahan. (He *has been exiting* in that door.)
Future Simple	*Maga*gua	*Magagua* sia sa sina nga puertahan. (He *will exit* in that door.)
Future Continuous	*Maga*gua	*Magagua* sia sa sina nga puertahan. (He *will be exiting* in that door.)
Future Perfect Simple	*Maga*gua *na*	*Magagua na* kuntani sia sa sina nga puertahan. (He *will have exited* in that door by then.)
Future Perfect Continuous	*Maga*gua *pa*	*Magagua pa* sia sa sina nga puertahan. (He *will have been exiting* in that door.)

30. To explain: paathag

Tenses	Word	Examples
Past Simple	*Nag*paathag	*Nagpaathag* sia sang rason. (She *explained* the reason.)
Past Continuous	*Nag*paathag	*Nagpaathag* sia sang rason. (She *was explaining* the reason.)
Past Perfect Simple	*Nag*paathag *na*	*Nagpaathag na* sia sang rason. (She *had explained* the reason.)
Past Perfect Continuous	*Nag*paathag *pa*	*Nagpaathag pa* sia sang rason. (She *had been explaining* the reason.)
Present Simple	*Naga*paathag	*Nagapaathag* sia sang rason. (She *explains* the reason.)
Present Continuous	*Naga*paathag	*Nagapaathag* sia sang rason. (She *is eplaining* the reason.)
Present Perfect Simple	*Naga*paathag *na*	*Nagapaathag na* sia sang rason. (She *has explained* the reason.)
Present Perfect Continuous	*Naga*paathag *pa*	*Nagapaathag pa* sia sang rason. (She *has been explaining* the reason.)
Future Simple	*Maga*paathag	*Magapaathag* sia sang rason. (She *will explain* the reason.)
Future Continuous	*Maga*paathag	*Magapaathag* sia sang rason. (She *will be explaining* the reason.)
Future Perfect Simple	*Maga*paathag *na*	*Magapaathag na* kuntani sia sang rason. (She *will have explained* the reason by then.)
Future Perfect Continuous	*Maga*paathag *pa*	*Magapaathag pa* sia sang rason. (She *will have been explaining* the reason.)

31. To fall: hulog, kahulog

Tenses	Word	Examples
Past Simple	_Na_hulog	_Nahulog_ ang mga dahon sa duta. (The leaves _fell_ on the ground.)
Past Continuous	_Naga_kahulog	_Nagakahulog_ ang mga dahon sa duta. (The leaves _were falling_ on the ground.)
Past Perfect Simple	_Na_hulog _na_	_Nahulog na_ ang mga dahon sa duta. (The leaves _had fallen_ on the ground.)
Past Perfect Continuous	_Naga_kahulog _pa_	_Nagakahulog pa_ ang mga dahon sa duta. (The leaves _had been falling_ on the ground.)
Present Simple	_Naga_kahulog	_Nagakahulog_ ang mga dahon sa duta. (The leaves _fall_ on the ground.)
Present Continuous	_Naga_kahulog	_Nagakahulog_ ang mga dahon sa duta. (The leaves _are falling_ on the ground.)
Present Perfect Simple	_Naga_kahulog _na_	_Nagakahulog na_ ang mga dahon sa duta. (The leaves _have fallen_ on the ground.)
Present Perfect Continuous	_Naga_kahulog _pa_	_Nagakahulog pa_ ang mga dahon sa duta. (The leaves _have been falling_ on the ground.)
Future Simple	_Ma_hulog	_Mahulog_ ang mga dahon sa duta. (The leaves _will fall_ on the ground.)
Future Continuous	_Ma_hulog	_Mahulog_ ang mga dahon sa duta. (The leaves _will be falling_ on the ground.)
Future Perfect Simple	_Ma_hulog _na_	_Mahulog na_ kuntani ang mga dahon sa duta. (The leaves _will have fallen_ on the ground by then.)
Future Perfect Continuous	_Ma_hulog _pa_	_Mahulog pa_ ang mga dahon sa duta. (The leaves _will have been falling_ on the ground.)

32. To feel: batyag

Tenses	Word	Examples
Past Simple	*Nag*batyag	*Nagbatyag* sia sang kasubo. (He *felt* sad.)
Past Continuous	*Nag*batyag	*Nagbatyag* sia sang kasubo. (He *was feeling* sad.)
Past Perfect Simple	*Nag*batyag *na*	*Nagbatyag na* sia sang kasubo. (He *had felt* sad.)
Past Perfect Continuous	*Nag*batyag *pa*	*Nagbatyag pa* sia sang kasubo. (He *had been feeling* sad.)
Present Simple	*Naga*batyag	*Nagabatyag* sia sang kasubo. (He *feels* sad.)
Present Continuous	*Naga*batyag	*Nagabatyag* sia sang kasubo. (He *is feeling* sad.)
Present Perfect Simple	*Naga*batyag *na*	*Nagabatyag na* sia sang kasubo. (He *has felt* sadn.)
Present Perfect Continuous	*Naga*batyag *pa*	*Nagabatyag pa* sia sang kasubo. (He *has been feeling* sad.)
Future Simple	*Maga*batyag	*Magabatyag* sia sang kasubo. (He *will feel* sad.)
Future Continuous	*Maga*batyag	*Magabatyag* sia sang kasubo. (He *will be feeling* sad.)
Future Perfect Simple	*Maga*batyag *na*	*Magabatyag na* kuntani sia sang kasubo. (He *will have felt* sad by then.)
Future Perfect Continuous	*Maga*batyag *pa*	*Magabatyag pa* sia sang kasubo. (He *will have been feeling* sad.)

33. To fight: away

Tenses	Word	Examples
Past Simple	**Nag**-away	*Nag-away* sila nga duha. (They *fought* each other.)
Past Continuous	**Nag**-away	*Nag-away* sila nga duha. (They *were fighting* each other.)
Past Perfect Simple	**Nag**-away **na**	*Nag-away na* sila nga duha. (They *had fought* each other.)
Past Perfect Continuous	**Nag**-away **pa**	*Nag-away pa* sila nga duha. (They *had been fighting* each other.)
Present Simple	**Naga**away	*Nagaaway* sila nga duha. (They *fight* each other.)
Present Continuous	**Naga**away	*Nagaaway* sila nga duha. (They *are fighting* each other.)
Present Perfect Simple	**Naga**away **na**	*Nagaaway na* sila nga duha. (They *have fought* each other.)
Present Perfect Continuous	**Naga**away **pa**	*Nagaaway pa* sila nga duha. (They *have been fighting* each other.)
Future Simple	**Maga**away	*Magaaway* sila nga duha. (They *will fight* each other.)
Future Continuous	**Maga**away	*Magaaway* sila nga duha. (They *will be fighting* each other.)
Future Perfect Simple	**Maga**away **na**	*Magaaway na* kuntani sila nga duha. (They *will have fought* each other by then.)
Future Perfect Continuous	**Maga**away **pa**	*Magaaway pa* sila nga duha. (They *will have been fighting* each other.)

34. To find: kita, pangita

Tenses	Word	Examples
Past Simple	*Na*kita	*Nakita* niya ang nadula nga sensilyo. (He *found* the lost coin.)
Past Continuous	*Gin*pangita	*Ginpangita* niya ang nadula nga sensilyo. (He *was finding* the lost coin.)
Past Perfect Simple	*Na*kita *na*	*Nakita na* niya ang nadula nga sensilyo. (He *had found* the lost coin.)
Past Perfect Continuous	*Gin*pangita *pa*	*Ginpangita pa* niya ang nadula nga sensilyo. (He *had been finding* the lost coin.)
Present Simple	*Na*kita	*Nakita* niya ang nadula nga sensilyo. (He *finds* the lost coin.)
Present Continuous	*Gina*pangita	*Ginapangita* niya ang nadula nga sensilyo. (He *is finding* the lost coin.)
Present Perfect Simple	*Na*kita *na*	*Nakita na* niya ang nadula nga sensilyo. (He *has found* the lost coin.)
Present Perfect Continuous	*Gina*pangita *pa*	*Ginapangita pa* niya ang nadula nga sensilyo. (He *has been finding* the lost coin.)
Future Simple	*Ma*kita	*Makita* niya ang nadula nga sensilyo. (He *will find* the lost coin.)
Future Continuous	*Maga*pangita	*Magapangita* sia sang nadula nga sensilyo. (He *will be finding* the lost coin.)
Future Perfect Simple	*Maga*pangita *na*	*Magapangita na* kuntani sia sang nadula nga sensilyo. (He *will have found* the lost coin by then.)
Future Perfect Continuous	*Maga*pangita *pa*	*Magapangita pa* sia sang nadula nga sensilyo. (He *will have been finding* the lost coin.)

35. To finish: tapos

Tenses	Word	Examples
Past Simple	**Gin**tapos	*Gintapos* niya ang iya obra. (He *finished* his work.)
Past Continuous	**Gin**tapos	*Gintapos* niya ang iya obra. (He *was finishing* his work.)
Past Perfect Simple	**Gin**tapos **na**	*Ginapos na* niya ang iya obra. (He *had finished* his work.)
Past Perfect Continuous	**Gin**tapos **pa**	*Gintapos pa* niya ang obra. (He *had been finishing* his work.)
Present Simple	**Gina**tapos	*Ginatapos* niya ang iya obra. (He *finishes* his work.)
Present Continuous	**Gina**tapos	*Ginatapos* niya ang iya obra. (He *is finishing* his work.)
Present Perfect Simple	**Gina**tapos **na**	*Ginatapos na* niya ang iya obra. (He *has finished* his work.)
Present Perfect Continuous	**Gina**tapos **pa**	*Ginatapos pa* niya ang iya obra. (He *has been finishing* his work.)
Future Simple	**Maga**tapos	*Magatapos* sia sang iya obra. (He *will finish* his work.)
Future Continuous	**Maga**tapos	*Magatapos* sia sang iya obra. (He *will be finishing* his work.)
Future Perfect Simple	**Maga**tapos **na**	*Magatapos na* kuntani sia sang iya obra. (He *will have finished* his work by then.)
Future Perfect Continuous	**Maga**tapos **pa**	*Magatapos pa* sia sang iya obra. (He *will have been finishing* his work.)

36

36. To fly: lupad

Tenses	Word	Examples
Past Simple	*Nag*lupad	*Naglupad* ang mga pispis. (The birds *flew*.)
Past Continuous	*Nag*lupad	*Naglupad* ang mga pispis. (The birds *were flying*.)
Past Perfect Simple	*Nag*lupad **na**	*Naglupad na* ang mga pispis. (The birds *had flown*.)
Past Perfect Continuous	*Nag*lupad **pa**	*Naglupad pa* ang mga pispis. (The birds *had been flying*.)
Present Simple	*Naga*lupad	*Nagalupad* ang mga pispis. (The birds *fly*.)
Present Continuous	*Naga*lupad	*Nagalupad* ang mga pispis. (The birds *are flying*.)
Present Perfect Simple	*Naga*lupad **na**	*Nagalupad na* ang mga pispis. (The birds *have flown*.)
Present Perfect Continuous	*Naga*lupad **pa**	*Nagalupad pa* ang mga pispis. (The birds *have been flying*.)
Future Simple	*Maga*lupad	*Magalupad* ang mga pispis. (The birds *will fly*.)
Future Continuous	*Maga*lupad	*Magalupad* ang mga psipis. (The birds *will be flying*.)
Future Perfect Simple	*Maga*lupad **na**	*Magalupad na* kuntani ang mga pispis. (The birds *will have flown* by then.)
Future Perfect Continuous	*Maga*lupad **pa**	*Magalupad pa* ang mga pispis. (The birds *will have been flying*.)

37. To forget: kalimtan

Tenses	Word	Examples
Past Simple	*Gin*kalimtan	*Ginkalimtan* ko ang akon promisa. (I *forgot* my promise.)
Past Continuous	*Gin*kalimtan	*Ginkalimtan* ko ang akon promisa. (I *was forgetting* my promise.)
Past Perfect Simple	*Gin*kalimtan *na*	*Ginkalimtan na* nakon ang akon promisa. (I *had forgotten* my promise.)
Past Perfect Continuous	*Gin*kalimtan *pa*	*Ginkalimtan pa* nakon ang akon promisa. (I *had been forgetting* my promise.)
Present Simple	*Gina*kalimtan	*Ginakalimtan* ko ang akon promisa. (I *forget* my promise.)
Present Continuous	*Gina*kalimtan	*Ginakalimtan* ko ang akon promisa. (I *am forgetting* my promise.)
Present Perfect Simple	*Gina*kalimtan *na*	*Ginakalimtan na* nakon ang akon problema. (I *have forgotten* my promise.)
Present Perfect Continuous	*Gina*kalimtan *pa*	*Ginakalimtan pa* nakon ang akon promisa. (I *have been forgetting* my promise.)
Future Simple	*Paga*kalimtan	*Pagakalimtan* ko ang akon promisa. (I *will forget* my promise.)
Future Continuous	*Paga*kalimtan	*Pagakalimtan* ko ang akon promisa. (I *will be forgetting* my promise.)
Future Perfect Simple	*Paga*kalimtan *na*	*Pagakalimtan na* nakon ang akon promisa. (I *will have forgotten* my promise by then.)
Future Perfect Continuous	*Paga*kalimtan *pa*	*Pagakalimtan pa* nakon ang akon promisa. (I *will have been forgetting* my promise.)

38. To get up: bangon

Tenses	Word	Examples
Past Simple	**Nag**bangon	*Nagbangon* ako aga pa. (I *got up* early in the morning.)
Past Continuous	**Nag**bangon	*Nagbangon* ako aga pa. (I *was getting up* early in the morning.)
Past Perfect Simple	**Nag**bangon **na**	*Nagbangon na* ako aga pa. (I *had got up* early in the morning.)
Past Perfect Continuous	**Nag**bangon **pa**	*Nagbangon pa* ako aga pa. (I *had been getting up* early in the morning.)
Present Simple	**Naga**bangon	*Nagabangon* ako aga pa. (I *get up* early in the morning.)
Present Continuous	**Naga**bangon	*Nagabangon* ako aga pa. (I *am getting up* early in the morning.)
Present Perfect Simple	**Naga**bangon **na**	*Nagabangon na* ako aga pa. (I *have got up* early in the morning.)
Present Perfect Continuous	**Naga**bangon **pa**	*Nagabangon pa* ako aga pa. (I *have been getting up* early in the morning.)
Future Simple	**Maga**bangon	*Magabangon* ako aga pa. (I *will get up* early in the morning.)
Future Continuous	**Maga**bangon	*Magabangon* ako aga pa. (I *will be getting up* early in the morning.)
Future Perfect Simple	**Maga**bangon **na**	*Magabangon na* kuntani ako aga pa. (I *will have got up* early in the morning by then.)
Future Perfect Continuous	**Maga**bangon **pa**	*Magabangon pa* ako aga pa. (I *will have been getting up* early in the morning.)

39. To give: hatag

Tenses	Word	Examples
Past Simple	_Nag_hatag	_Naghatag_ ako sang tion para magtuon. (I _gave_ time to study.)
Past Continuous	_Nag_hatag	_Naghatag_ ako sang tion para magtuon. (I _was giving_ time to study.)
Past Perfect Simple	_Nag_hatag _na_	_Naghatag na_ ako sang tion para magtuon. (I _had given_ time to study.)
Past Perfect Continuous	_Nag_hatag _pa_	_Naghatag pa_ ako sang tion para magtuon. (I _had been giving_ time to study.)
Present Simple	_Naga_hatag	_Nagahatag_ ako sang tion para magtuon. (I _give_ time to study.)
Present Continuous	_Naga_hatag	_Nagahatag_ ako sang tion para magtuon. (I _am giving_ time to study.)
Present Perfect Simple	_Naga_hatag _na_	_Nagahatag na_ ako sang tion para magtuon. (I _have given_ time to study.)
Present Perfect Continuous	_Naga_hatag _pa_	_Nagahatag pa_ ako sang tion para magtuon. (I _have been giving_ time to study.)
Future Simple	_Maga_hatag	_Magahatag_ ako sang tion para magtuon. (I _will give_ time to study.)
Future Continuous	_Maga_hatag	_Magahatag_ ako sang tion para magtuon. (I _will be giving_ time to study.)
Future Perfect Simple	_Maga_hatag _na_	_Magahatag na_ kuntani ako sang tion para magtuon. (I _will have given_ time to study by then.)
Future Perfect Continuous	_Maga_hatag _pa_	_Magahatag pa_ ako sang tion para magtuon. (I _will have been giving_ time to study.)

40. To go: kadto

Tenses	Word	Examples
Past Simple	_Nag_kadto	_Nagkadto_ ako sa merkado. (I _went_ to the market.)
Past Continuous	_Nag_kadto	_Nagkadto_ ako sa merkado. (I _was going_ to the market.)
Past Perfect Simple	_Nag_kadto _na_	_Nagkadto na_ ako sa merkado. (I _had gone_ to the market.)
Past Perfect Continuous	_Nag_kadto _pa_	_Nagkadto pa_ ako sa merkado. (I _had been going_ to the market.)
Present Simple	_Naga_kadto	_Nagakadto_ ako sa merkado. (I _go_ to the market.)
Present Continuous	_Naga_kadto	_Nagakadto_ ako sa merkado. (I _am going_ to the market.)
Present Perfect Simple	_Naga_kadto _na_	_Nagakadto na_ ako sa merkado. (I _have gone_ to the market.)
Present Perfect Continuous	_Naga_kadto _pa_	_Nagakadto pa_ ako sa merkado. (I _have been going_ to the market.)
Future Simple	_Maga_kadto	_Magakadto_ ako sa merkado. (I _will go_ to the market.)
Future Continuous	_Maga_kadto	_Magakadto_ ako sa merkado. (I _will be going_ to the market.)
Future Perfect Simple	_Maga_kadto _na_	_Magakadto na_ kuntani ako sa merkado. (I _will have gone_ to the market by then.)
Future Perfect Continuous	_Maga_kadto _pa_	_Magakadto pa_ ako sa merkado. (I _will have been going_ to the market.)

41. To happen: tabo, katabo

Tenses	Word	Examples
Past Simple	*Na*tabo	Ano ang *natabo* sa iya? (What *happened* to her?)
Past Continuous	*Na*tabo	Ano ang *natabo* sa iya? (What *was happening* to her?)
Past Perfect Simple	*Na*tabo *na*	Ano ang *natabo na* sa iya? (What *had happened* to her.)
Past Perfect Continuous	*Na*tabo *pa*	Ano ang *natabo pa* sa iya? (What *had been happening* to her?)
Present Simple	*Naga*katabo	Ano ang *nagakatabo* sa iya? (What *happens* to her?)
Present Continuous	*Naga*katabo	Ano ang *nagakatabo* sa iya? (What *is happening* to her?)
Present Perfect Simple	*Naga*katabo *na*	Ano ang *nagakatabo na* sa iya? (What *has happened* to her?)
Present Perfect Continuous	*Naga*katabo *pa*	Ano ang *nagakatabo pa* sa iya? (What *has been happening* to her?)
Future Simple	*Ma*tabo	Ano ang *matabo* sa iya? (What *will happen* to her?)
Future Continuous	*Ma*tabo	Ano ang *matabo* sa iya? (What *will be happening* to her?)
Future Perfect Simple	*Ma*tabo *na*	Ano ang *matabo na* kuntani sa iya? (What *will have happened* to her by then?)
Future Perfect Continuous	*Ma*tabo *pa*	Ano ang *matabo pa* sa iya? (What *will have been happening* to her?)

42. To have: na, naga

Tenses	Word	Examples
Past Simple	_**Na**_	_Na_mahaw ka na? (Have you _had_ breakfast?)
Past Continuous	No equivalent	No equivalent
Past Perfect Simple	No equivalent	No equivalent
Past Perfect Continuous	No equivalent	No equivalent
Present Simple	_**Naga**_	_Naga_pamahaw ka? (_Have_ you breakfasted?)
Present Continuous	No equivalent	No equivalent
Present Perfect Simple	No equivalent	No equivalent
Present Perfect Continuous	No equivalent	No equivalent
Future Simple	No equivalent	No equivalent
Future Continuous	No equivalent	No equivalent
Future Perfect Simple	No equivalent	No equivalent
Future Perfect Continuous	No equivalent	No equivalent

43. To hear: bati, batian, pamatian

Tenses	Word	Examples
Past Simple	*Na*batian	*Nabatian* ko ang iya ginasiling. (I *heard* what she said.)
Past Continuous	*Gin*pamatian	*Ginpamatian* ko ang iya ginasiling. (I *was hearing* what she said.)
Past Perfect Simple	*Na*batian *na*	*Nabatian na* nakon ang iya ginasiling. (I *had heard* what she said.)
Past Perfect Continuous	*Gin*pamatian *pa*	*Ginpamatian pa* nakon ang iya ginasiling. (I *had been hearing* what she said.)
Present Simple	*Na*batian	*Nabatian* ko ang iya ginasiling. (I *hear* what she says.)
Present Continuous	*Gina*pamatian	*Ginapamatian* ko ang iya ginasiling. (I *am hearing* what she is saying.)
Present Perfect Simple	*Na*batian *na*	*Nabatian na* nakon ang iya ginasiling. (I *have heard* what she said.)
Present Perfect Continuous	*Gina*pamatian *pa*	*Ginapamatian pa* ko ang iya ginasiling. (I *have been hearing* what she is saying.)
Future Simple	*Paga*pamatian	*Pagapamatian* ko ang iya ginasiling. (I *will hear* what she says.)
Future Continuous	*Paga*pamatian	*Pagapamatian* ko ang iya ginasiling. (I *will be hearing* what she says.)
Future Perfect Simple	*Paga*pamatian *na*	*Pagapamatian na* kuntani nakon ang iya ginasiling. (I *will have heard* what she says by then.)
Future Perfect Continuous	*Paga*pamatian *pa*	*Pagapamatian pa* nakon ang iya ginasiling. (I *will have been hearing* what she says.)

44. To help: bulig, buligan

Tenses	Word	Examples
Past Simple	_**Gin**_buligan	_Ginbuligan_ niya ako sa pagkay-o sang salakyan. (He _helped_ me repair the car.)
Past Continuous	_**Gin**_buligan	_Ginbuligan_ niya ako sa pagkay-o sang salakyan. (He _was helping_ me repair the car.)
Past Perfect Simple	_**Gin**_buligan _**na**_	_Ginbuligan na_ niya ako sa pagkay-o sang salakyan. (He _had helped_ me repair the car.)
Past Perfect Continuous	_**Gin**_buligan _**pa**_	_Ginbuligan pa_ niya ako sa pagkay-o sang salakyan. (He _had been helping_ me repair the car.)
Present Simple	_**Gina**_buligan	_Ginabuligan_ niya ako sa pagkay-o sang salakyan. (He _helps_ me repair the car.)
Present Continuous	_**Gina**_buligan	_Ginabuligan_ niya ako sa pagkay-o sang salakyan. (He _is helping_ me repair the car.)
Present Perfect Simple	_**Gina**_buligan _**na**_	_Ginabuligan na_ niya ako sa pagkay-o sang salakyan. (He _has helped_ me repair the car.)
Present Perfect Continuous	_**Gina**_buligan _**pa**_	_Ginabuligan pa_ niya ako sa pagkay-o sang salakyan. (He _has been helping_ me repair the car.)
Future Simple	_**Maga**_bulig	_Magabulig_ sia sa akon sa pagkay-o sang salakyan. (He _will help_ me repair the car.)
Future Continuous	_**Maga**_bulig	_Magabulig_ sia sa akon sa pagkay-o sang salakyan. (He _will be helping_ me to repair the car.)
Future Perfect Simple	_**Maga**_bulig _**na**_	_Magabulig na_ kuntani sia sa akon sa pagkay-o sang salakyan. (He _will have helped_ me repair the car by then.)

Future Perfect Continuous	*Maga*bulig *pa*	*Magabulig pa* sia sa akon sa pagkay-o sang salakyan. (He *will have been helping* me repair the car.)

45. To hold: uyat, uyatan

Tenses	Word	Examples
Past Simple	*Gin*-uyatan	*Gin-uyatan* niya ang bata. (He *held* the child.)
Past Continuous	*Gin*-uyatan	*Gin-uyatan* niya ang bata. (He *was holding* the child.)
Past Perfect Simple	*Gin*-uyatan *na*	*Gin-uyatan na* niya ang bata. (He *had held* the child.)
Past Perfect Continuous	*Gin*-uyatan *pa*	*Gin-uyatan pa* niya ang bata. (He *had been holding* the child.)
Present Simple	*Gina*uyatan	*Ginauyatan* niya ang bata. (He *holds* the child.)
Present Continuous	*Gina*uyatan	*Ginauyatan* niya ang bata. (He *is holding* the child.)
Present Perfect Simple	*Gina*uyatan *na*	*Ginauyatan na* niya ang bata. (He *has held* the child.)
Present Perfect Continuous	*Gina*uyatan *pa*	*Ginauyatan pa* niya ang bata. (He *has been holding* the child.)
Future Simple	*Maga*uyat	*Magauyat* sia sang bata. (He *willhold* the child.)
Future Continuous	*Maga*uyat	*Magauyat* sia sang bata. (He *will be holding* the child.)
Future Perfect Simple	*Maga*uyat *na*	*Magauyat na* kuntani sia sang bata. (He *will have held* the child by then.)
Future Perfect Continuous	*Maga*uyat *pa*	*Magauyat pa* sia sang bata. (He *will have been holding* the child.)

46. To increase: dugang

Tenses	Word	Examples
Past Simple	*Nag*dugang	*Nagdugang* ang ila kadamuon. (They *increased* in number.)
Past Continuous	*Nag*dugang	*Nagdugang* ang ila kadamuon. (They *were increasing* in number.)
Past Perfect Simple	*Nag*dugang *na*	*Nagdugang na* ang ila kadamuon. (They *had increased* in number.)
Past Perfect Continuous	*Nag*dugang *pa*	*Nagdugang pa* ang ila kadamuon. (They *had been increasing* in number.)
Present Simple	*Naga*dugang	*Nagadugang* ang ila kadamuon. (They *increase* in number.)
Present Continuous	*Naga*dugang	*Nagadugang* ang ila kadamuon. (They *are increasing* in number.)
Present Perfect Simple	*Naga*dugang *na*	*Nagadugang na* ang ila kadamuon. (They *have increased* in number.)
Present Perfect Continuous	*Naga*dugang *pa*	*Nagadugang pa* ang ila kadamuon. (They *have been increasing* in number.)
Future Simple	*Maga*dugang	*Magadugang* ang ila kadamuon. (They *will increase* in number.)
Future Continuous	*Maga*dugang	*Magadugang* ang ila kadamuon. (They *will be increasing* in number.)
Future Perfect Simple	*Maga*dugang *na*	*Magadugang na* kuntani ang ila kadamuon. (They *will have increased* in number by then.)
Future Perfect Continuous	*Maga*dugang *pa*	*Magadugang pa* ang ila kadamuon. (They *will have been increasing* in number.)

47. To introduce: pakilala

Tenses	Word	Examples
Past Simple	**Nag**pakilala	*Nagpakilala* ako sa ila. (I *introduced* myself to them.)
Past Continuous	**Nag**pakilala	*Nagpakilala* ako sa ila. (I *was introducing* myself to them.)
Past Perfect Simple	**Nag**pakilala **na**	*Nagpakilala na* ako sa ila. (I *had introduced* myself to them.)
Past Perfect Continuous	**Nag**pakilala **pa**	*Nagpakilala pa* ako sa ila. (I *had been introducing* myself to them.)
Present Simple	**Naga**pakilala	*Nagapakilala* ako sa ila. (I *introduce* myself to them.)
Present Continuous	**Naga**pakilala	*Nagapakilala* ako sa ila. (I *am introducing* myself to them.)
Present Perfect Simple	**Naga**pakilala **na**	*Nagapakilala na* ako sa ila. (I *have introduced* myself to them.)
Present Perfect Continuous	**Naga**pakilala **pa**	*Nagapakilala pa* ako sa ila. (I *have been introducing* myself to them.)
Future Simple	**Maga**pakilala	*Magapakilala* ako sa ila. (I *will introduce* myself to them.)
Future Continuous	**Maga**pakilala	*Magapakilala* ako sa ila. (I *will be introducing* myself to them.)
Future Perfect Simple	**Maga**pakilala **na**	*Magapakilala na* kuntani ako sa ila. (I *will have introduced* myself to them by then.)
Future Perfect Continuous	**Maga**pakilala **pa**	*Magapakilala pa* ako sa ila. (I *will have been introducing* myself to them.)

48. To invite: agda

Tenses	Word	Examples
Past Simple	**Gin**-agda	*Gin-agda* niya sila. (He *invited them*.)
Past Continuous	**Gin**-agda	*Gin-agda* niya sila. (He *was inviting* them.)
Past Perfect Simple	**Gin**-agda **na**	*Gin-agda na* niya sila. (He *had invited* them.)
Past Perfect Continuous	**Gin**-agda **pa**	*Gin-agda pa* niya sila. (He *had been inviting* them.)
Present Simple	**Gina**agda	*Ginaagda* niya sila. (He *invites* them.)
Present Continuous	**Gina**agda	*Ginaagda* niya sila. (He *is inviting* them.)
Present Perfect Simple	**Gina**agda **na**	*Ginaagda na* niya sila. (He *has invited* them.)
Present Perfect Continuous	**Gina**agda **pa**	*Ginaagda pa* niya sila. (He *has been inviting* them.)
Future Simple	**Maga**agda	*Magaagda* sia sa ila. (He *will invite* them.)
Future Continuous	**Maga**agda	*Magaagda* sia sa ila. (He *will be inviting* them.)
Future Perfect Simple	**Maga**agda **na**	*Magaagda na* kuntani sia sa ila. (He *will have invited* them by then.)
Future Perfect Continuous	**Maga**agda **pa**	*Magaagda pa* sia sa ila. (He *will have been inviting* them.)

49. To kill: patay

Tenses	Word	Examples
Past Simple	**Gin**patay	*Ginpatay* nila ang sapat. (They *killed* the animal.)
Past Continuous	**Gin**patay	*Ginpatay* nila ang sapat. (The *were killing* the animal.)
Past Perfect Simple	**Gin**patay **na**	*Ginpatay na* nila ang sapat. (They *had killed* the animal.)
Past Perfect Continuous	**Gin**patay **pa**	*Ginpatay pa* nila ang sapat. (They *had been killing* the animal.)
Present Simple	**Gina**patay	*Ginapatay* nila ang sapat. (They *kill* the animal.)
Present Continuous	**Gina**patay	*Ginapatay* nila ang sapat. (They *are killing* the animal.)
Present Perfect Simple	**Gina**patay **na**	*Ginapatay na* nila ang sapat. (They *have killed* the animal.)
Present Perfect Continuous	**Gina**patay **pa**	*Ginapatay pa* nila ang sapat. (They *have been killing* the animal.)
Future Simple	**Maga**patay	*Magapatay* sila sang sapat. (They *will kill* the animal.)
Future Continuous	**Maga**patay	*Magapatay* sila sang sapat. (They *will be killing* the animal.)
Future Perfect Simple	**Maga**patay **na**	*Magapatay na* kuntani sila sang sapat. (They *will have killed* the animal by then.)
Future Perfect Continuous	**Maga**patay **pa**	*Magapatay pa* sila sang sapat. (They *will have been killing* the animal.)

50. To kiss: halok, halukan

Tenses	Word	Examples
Past Simple	*Gin*halukan	*Ginhalukan* sang iloy ang iya lapsag. (The mother *kissed* her baby.)
Past Continuous	*Gin*halukan	*Ginhalukan* sang iloy ang iya lapsag. (The mother *was kissing* her baby.)
Past Perfect Simple	*Gin*halukan *na*	*Ginhalukan na* sang iloy ang iya lapsag. (The mother *had kissed* her baby.)
Past Perfect Continuous	*Gin*halukan *pa*	*Ginhalukan pa* sang iloy ang iya lapsag. (The mother *had been kissing* her baby.)
Present Simple	*Gina*halukan	*Ginahalukan* sang iloy ang iya lapsag. (The mother *kisses* her baby.)
Present Continuous	*Gina*halukan	*Ginahalukan* sang iloy ang iya lapsag. (The mother *is kissing* her baby.)
Present Perfect Simple	*Gina*halukan *na*	*Ginahalukan na* sang iloy ang iya lapsag. (The mother *has kissed* her baby.)
Present Perfect Continuous	*Gina*halukan *pa*	*Ginahalukan pa* sang iloy ang iya lapsag. (The mother *has been kissing* her baby.)
Future Simple	*Maga*halok	*Magahalok* ang iloy sa iya lapsag. (The mother *will kiss* her baby.)
Future Continuous	*Maga*halok	*Magahalok* ang iloy sa iya lapsag. (The mother *will be kissing* her baby.)
Future Perfect Simple	*Maga*halok *na*	*Magahalok na* kuntani ang iloy sa iya lapsag. (The mother *will have kissed* her baby by then.)
Future Perfect Continuous	*Maga*halok *pa*	*Magahalok pa* ang iloy sa iya lapsag. (The mother *will have been kissing* her baby.)

51. To know: hibalo, hibaluan

Tenses	Word	Examples
Past Simple	*Na*hibaluan	*Nahibaluan* ko ang natabo. (I *knew* what happened.)
Past Continuous	*Gin*hibalo	*Ginhibalo* ko ang natabo. (I *was knowing* what happened.)
Past Perfect Simple	*Na*hibaluan *na*	*Nahibaluan na* nakon ang natabo. (I *had known* what happened.)
Past Perfect Continuous	*Gin*hibalo *pa*	*Ginhibalo pa* nakon ang natabo. (I *had been knowing* what happened.)
Present Simple	*Naka*hibalo	*Nakahibalo* ako sang natabo. (I *know* what happened.)
Present Continuous	*Gina*hibalo	*Ginahibalo* ko ang natabo. (I *am knowing* what happened.)
Present Perfect Simple	*Na*hibaluan *na*	*Nahibaluan na* nakon ang natabo. (I *have known* what happened.)
Present Perfect Continuous	*Gina*hibalo *pa*	*Ginahibalo pa* nakon ang natabo. (I *have been knowing* what happened.)
Future Simple	*Ma*hibaluan	*Mahibaluan* ko ang natabo. (I *will know* what happened.)
Future Continuous	*Ma*hibaluan	*Mahibaluan* ko ang natabo. (I *will be knowing* what happened.)
Future Perfect Simple	*Maga*hibalo *na*	*Mahibaluan na* kuntani nakon ang natabo. (I *will have known* what happened by then.)
Future Perfect Continuous	*Ma*hibaluan *pa*	*Mahibaluan pa* nakon ang natabo. (I *will have been knowing* what happened.)

52. To laugh: kadlaw

Tenses	Word	Examples
Past Simple	*Nag*kadlaw	*Nagkadlaw* ang lapsag. (The baby *laughed*.)
Past Continuous	*Nag*kadlaw	*Nagkadlaw* ang lapsag. (The baby *was laughing*.)
Past Perfect Simple	*Nag*kadlaw *na*	*Nagkadlaw na* ang lapsag. (The baby *had laughed*.)
Past Perfect Continuous	*Nag*kadlaw *pa*	*Nagkadlaw pa* ang lapsag. (The baby *had been laughing*.)
Present Simple	*Naga*kadlaw	*Nagakadlaw* ang lapsag. (The baby *laughs*.)
Present Continuous	*Naga*kadlaw	*Nagakadlaw* ang lapsag. (The baby *is laughing*.)
Present Perfect Simple	*Naga*kadlaw *na*	*Nagakadlaw na* ang lapsag. (The baby *has laughed*.)
Present Perfect Continuous	*Naga*kadlaw *pa*	*Nagakadlaw pa* ang lapsag. (The baby *has been laughing*.)
Future Simple	*Maga*kadlaw	*Magakadlaw* ang lapsag. (The baby *will laugh*.)
Future Continuous	*Maga*kadlaw	*Magakadlaw* ang lapsag. (The baby *will be laughing*.)
Future Perfect Simple	*Maga*kadlaw *na*	*Magakadlaw na* kuntani ang lapsag. (The baby *will have laughed* by then.)
Future Perfect Continuous	*Maga*kadlaw *pa*	*Magakadlaw pa* ang lapsag. (The baby *will have been laughing*.)

53. To learn: tuon

Tenses	Word	Examples
Past Simple	**Nag**tuon	*Nagtuon* ako parte sa Biblia. (I *learned* about the Bible.)
Past Continuous	**Nag**tuon	*Nagtuon* ako parte sa Biblia. (I *was learning* about the Bible.)
Past Perfect Simple	**Nag**tuon *na*	*Nagtuon na* ako parte sa Biblia. (I *had learned* about the Bible.)
Past Perfect Continuous	**Nag**tuon *pa*	*Nagtuon pa* ako parte sa Biblia. (I *had been learning* about the Bible.)
Present Simple	**Naga**tuon	*Nagatuon* ako parte sa Biblia. (I *learn* about the Bible.)
Present Continuous	**Naga**tuon	*Nagatuon* ako parte sa Biblia. (I *am learning* about the Bible.)
Present Perfect Simple	**Naga**tuon *na*	*Nagatuon na* ako parte sa Biblia. (I *have learned* about the Bible.)
Present Perfect Continuous	**Naga**tuon *pa*	*Nagatuon pa* ako parte sa Biblia. (I *have been learning* about the Bible.)
Future Simple	**Maga**tuon	*Magatuon* ako parte sa Biblia. (I *will learn* about the Bible.)
Future Continuous	**Maga**tuon	*Magatuon* ako parte sa Biblia. (I *will be learning* about the Bible.)
Future Perfect Simple	**Maga**tuon *na*	*Magatuon na* kuntani ako parte sa Biblia. (I *will have learned* about the Bible by then.)
Future Perfect Continuous	**Maga**tuon *pa*	*Magatuon pa* ako parte sa Biblia. (I *will have been learning* about the Bible.)

54. To lie down: higda

Tenses	Word	Examples
Past Simple	*Nag*higda	*Naghigda* sia sa katre. (He *lied down* in bed.)
Past Continuous	*Nag*higda	*Naghigda* sia sa katre. (He *was lying down* in bed.)
Past Perfect Simple	*Nag*higda *na*	*Naghigda na* sia sa katre. (He *had lied down* in bed.)
Past Perfect Continuous	*Nag*higda *pa*	*Naghigda pa* sia sa katre. (He *had been lying down* in bed.)
Present Simple	*Naga*higda	*Nagahigda* sia sa katre. (He *lies down* in bed.)
Present Continuous	*Naga*higda	*Nagahigda* sia sa katre. (He *is lying down* in bed.)
Present Perfect Simple	*Naga*higda *na*	*Nagahigda na* sia sa katre. (He *has lied down* in bed.)
Present Perfect Continuous	*Naga*higda *pa*	*Nagahigda pa* sia sa katre. (He *has been lying down* in bed.)
Future Simple	*Maga*higda	*Magahigda* sia sa katre. (He *will lie down* in bed.)
Future Continuous	*Maga*higda	*Magahigda* sia sa katre. (He *will be lying down* in bed.)
Future Perfect Simple	*Maga*higda *na*	*Magahigda na* kuntani sia sa katre. (He *will have lied down* in bed.)
Future Perfect Continuous	*Maga*higda *pa*	*Magahigda pa* sia sa katre. (He *will have been lying down* in bed.)

55. To like: gustuhan

Tenses	Word	Examples
Past Simple	_Na_gustuhan	_Nagustuhan_ niya ang luto. (He _liked_ the menu.)
Past Continuous	_Na_gustuhan	_Nagustuhan_ niya ang luto. (He _was liking_ the menu.)
Past Perfect Simple	_Na_gustuhan _na_	_Nagustuhan na_ niya ang luto. (He _had liked_ the menu.)
Past Perfect Continuous	_Na_gustuhan _pa_	_Nagustuhan pa_ niya ang luto. (He _had been liking_ the menu.)
Present Simple	_Na_gustuhan	_Nagustuhan_ niya ang luto. (He _likes_ the menu.)
Present Continuous	_Na_gustuhan	_Nagustuhan_ niya ang luto. (He _is liking_ the menu.)
Present Perfect Simple	_Na_gustuhan _na_	_Nagustuhan na_ niya ang luto. (He _has liked_ the menu.)
Present Perfect Continuous	_Na_gustuhan _pa_	_Nagustuhan pa_ niya ang luto. (He _has been liking_ the menu.)
Future Simple	_Ma_gustuhan	_Magustuhan_ niya ang luto. (He _will like_ the menu.)
Future Continuous	_Ma_gustuhan	_Magustuhan_ niya ang luto. (He _will be liking_ the menu.)
Future Perfect Simple	_Ma_gustuhan _na_	_Magustuhan na_ kuntani niya ang luto. (He _will have liked_ the menu by then.)
Future Perfect Continuous	_Ma_gustuhan _pa_	_Magustuhan pa_ niya ang luto. (He _will have been liking_ the menu.)

56. To listen: pamati

Tenses	Word	Examples
Past Simple	**Nag**pamati	*Nagpamati* sia sang musika. (He *listened* to the music.)
Past Continuous	**Nag**pamati	*Nagpamati* sia sang musika. (He *was listening* to the music.)
Past Perfect Simple	**Nag**pamati **na**	*Nagpamati na* sia sang musika. (He *had listened* to the music.)
Past Perfect Continuous	**Nag**pamati **pa**	*Nagpamati pa* sia sang musika. (He *had been listening* to the music.)
Present Simple	**Naga**pamati	*Nagapamati* sia sang musika. (He *listens* to the music.)
Present Continuous	**Naga**pamati	*Nagapamati* sia sang musika. (He *is listening* to the music.)
Present Perfect Simple	**Naga**pamati **na**	*Nagapamati na* sia sang musika. (He *has listened* to the music.)
Present Perfect Continuous	**Naga**pamati **pa**	*Nagapamati pa* sia sang musika. (He *has been listening* to the music.)
Future Simple	**Maga**pamati	*Magapamati* sia sang musika. (He *will listen* to the music.)
Future Continuous	**Maga**pamati	*Magapamati* sia sang musika. (He *will be listening* to the music.)
Future Perfect Simple	**Maga**pamati **na**	*Magapamati na* kuntani sia sang musika. (He *will have listened* to the music by then.)
Future Perfect Continuous	**Maga**pamati **pa**	*Magapamati pa* sia sang musika. (He *will have been listening* to the music.)

57. To live: kabuhi

Tenses	Word	Examples
Past Simple	*Nag*kabuhi	*Nagkabuhi* kita sa katapusan nga mga adlaw. (We *lived* in the last days.)
Past Continuous	*Nag*kabuhi	*Nagkabuhi* kita sa katapusan nga mga adlaw. (We *were living* in the last days.)
Past Perfect Simple	*Nag*kabuhi *na*	*Nagkabuhi na* kita sa katapusan nga mga adlaw. (We *had lived* in the last days.)
Past Perfect Continuous	*Nag*kabuhi *pa*	*Nagkabuhi pa* kita sa katapusan nga mga adlaw. (We *had been living* in the last days.)
Present Simple	*Naga*kabuhi	*Nagakabuhi* kita sa katapusan nga mga adlaw. (We *live* in the last days.)
Present Continuous	*Naga*kabuhi	*Nagakabuhi* kita sa katapusan nga mga adlaw. (We *are living* in the last days.)
Present Perfect Simple	*Naga*kabuhi *na*	*Nagakabuhi na* kita sa katapusan nga mga adlaw. (We *have lived* in the last days.)
Present Perfect Continuous	*Naga*kabuhi *pa*	*Nagakabuhi pa* kita sa katapusan nga mga adlaw. (We *have been living* in the last days.)
Future Simple	*Maga*kabuhi	*Magakabuhi* kita sa katapusan nga mga adlaw. (We *will live* in the last days.)
Future Continuous	*Maga*kabuhi	*Magakabuhi* kita sa katapusan nga mga adlaw. (We *will be living* in the last days.)
Future Perfect Simple	*Maga*kabuhi *na*	*Magakabuhi na* kuntani kita sa katapusan nga mga adlaw. (We *will have lived* in the last days by then.)
Future Perfect Continuous	*Maga*kabuhi *pa*	*Magakabuhi pa* kita sa katapusan nga mga adlaw. (We *will have been living* in the last days.)

58. To lose: dula

Tenses	Word	Examples
Past Simple	_Na_dula	_Nadula_ niya ang iya pagkabutang. (He _lost_ his belongings.)
Past Continuous	_Gin_dula	_Gindula_ niya ang iya pagkabutang. (He _was losing_ his belongings.)
Past Perfect Simple	_Na_dula _na_	_Nadula na_ niya ang iya pagkabutang. (He _had lost_ his belongings.)
Past Perfect Continuous	_Gin_dula _pa_	_Gindula pa_ niya ang iya pagkabutang. (He _had been losing_ his belongings.)
Present Simple	_Na_dula	_Nadula_ niya ang iya pagkabutang. (He _loses_ his belongings.)
Present Continuous	_Gina_dula	_Ginadula_ niya ang iya pagkabutang. (He _is losing_ his belongings.)
Present Perfect Simple	_Na_dula _na_	_Nadula na_ niya ang iya pagkabutang. (He _has lost_ his belongings.)
Present Perfect Continuous	_Gina_dula _pa_	_Ginadula pa_ niya ang iya pagkabutang. (He _has been losing_ his belongings.)
Future Simple	_Ma_dula	_Madula_ niya ang iya pagkabutang. (He _will lose_ his belongings.)
Future Continuous	_Ma_dula	_Madula_ niya ang iya pagkabutang. (He _will be losing_ his belongings.)
Future Perfect Simple	_Ma_dula _na_	_Madula na_ kuntani niya ang iya pagkabutang. (He _will have lost_ his belongings by then.)
Future Perfect Continuous	_Ma_dula _pa_	_Madula pa_ niya ang iya pagkabutang. (He _will have been losing_ his belongings.)

59. To love: higugma, higugmaon

Tenses	Word	Examples
Past Simple	**Gin**higugma	*Ginhigugma* niya ako. (He *loved* me.)
Past Continuous	**Gin**higugma	*Ginhigugma* niya ako. (He *was loving* me.)
Past Perfect Simple	**Gin**higugma **na**	*Ginhigugma na* niya ako. (He *had loved* me.)
Past Perfect Continuous	**Gin**higugma **pa**	*Ginhigugma pa* niya ako. (He *had been loving* me.)
Present Simple	**Gina**higugma	*Ginahigugma* niya ako. (He *loves* me.)
Present Continuous	**Gina**higugma	*Ginahigugma* niya ako (He *is loving* me.)
Present Perfect Simple	**Gina**higugma **na**	*Ginahigugma na* niya ako (He *has loved* me.)
Present Perfect Continuous	**Gina**higugma **pa**	*Ginahigugma pa* niya ako. (He *has been loving* me.)
Future Simple	**Paga**higugmaon	*Pagahigugmaon* niya ako. (He *will love* me.)
Future Continuous	**Paga**higugmaon	*Pagahigugmaon* niya ako. (He *will be loving* me.)
Future Perfect Simple	**Paga**higugmaon **na**	*Pagahigugmaon na* kuntani niya ako. (He *will have loved* me by then.)
Future Perfect Continuous	**Paga**higugmaon **pa**	*Pagahigugmaon pa* niya ako. (He *will have been loving* me.)

60. To meet: sugata

Tenses	Word	Examples
Past Simple	*Nag*sugata	*Nagsugata* sila sa amon. (They *met* us.)
Past Continuous	*Nag*sugata	*Nagsugata* sila sa amon. (They *were meeting* us.)
Past Perfect Simple	*Nag*sugata *na*	*Nagsugata na* sila sa amon. (They *had met* us.)
Past Perfect Continuous	*Nag*sugata *pa*	*Nagsugata pa* sila sa amon. (They *had been meeting* us.)
Present Simple	*Naga*sugata	*Nagasugata* sila sa amon. (They *meet* us.)
Present Continuous	*Naga*sugata	*Nagasugata* sila sa amon. (They *are meeting* us.)
Present Perfect Simple	*Naga*sugata *na*	*Nagasugata na* sila sa amon. (They *have met* us.)
Present Perfect Continuous	*Naga*sugata *pa*	*Nagasugata pa* sila sa amon. (They *have been meeting* us.)
Future Simple	*Maga*sugata	*Magasugata* sila sa amon. (They *will meet* us.)
Future Continuous	*Maga*sugata	*Magasugata* sila sa amon. (They *will be meeting* us.)
Future Perfect Simple	*Maga*sugata *na*	*Magasugata na* kuntani sila sa amon. (They *will have met* us by then.)
Future Perfect Continuous	*Maga*sugata *pa*	*Magasugata pa* sila sa amon. (They *will have been meeting* us.)

61. To need: kinahanglan

Tenses	Word	Examples
Past Simple	*Nag*kinahanglan	*Nagkinahanglan* sia sang bulig. (He *needed* help.)
Past Continuous	*Nag*kinahanglan	*Nagkinahanglan* sia sang bulig. (He *was needing* help.)
Past Perfect Simple	*Nag*kinahanglan *na*	*Nagkinahanglan na* sia sang bulig. (He *had needed* help.)
Past Perfect Continuous	*Nag*kinahanglan *pa*	*Nagkinahanglan pa* sia sang bulig. (He *had been needing* help.)
Present Simple	*Naga*kinahanglan	*Nagakinahanglan* sia sang bulig. (He *needs* help.)
Present Continuous	*Naga*kinahanglan	*Nagkinahanglan* sia sang bulig. (He *is needing* help.)
Present Perfect Simple	*Naga*kinahanglan *na*	*Nagakinahanglan na* sia sang bulig. (He *has needed* help.)
Present Perfect Continuous	*Naga*kinahanglan *pa*	*Nagakinahanglan pa* sia sang bulig. (He *has been needing* help.)
Future Simple	*Maga*kinahanglan	*Magakinahanglan* sia sang bulig. (He *will need* help.)
Future Continuous	*Maga*kinahanglan	*Magakinahanglan* sia sang bulig. (He *will be needing* help.)
Future Perfect Simple	*Maga*kinahanglan *na*	*Magakinahanglan na* kuntani sia sang bulig. (He *will have needed* help by then.)
Future Perfect Continuous	*Maga*kinahanglan *pa*	*Magakinahanglan pa* sia sang bulig. (He *will have been needing* help.)

62. To notice: talupangdan, talupangod, talupangdon

Tenses	Word	Examples
Past Simple	_Na_talupangdan	_Natalupangdan_ nila nga maluya ako. (They _noticed_ that I am weak.)
Past Continuous	_Gin_talupangod	_Gintalupangod_ nila nga maluya ako. (They _were noticing_ that I am weak.)
Past Perfect Simple	_Na_talupangdan _na_	_Natalupangdan na_ nila nga maluya ako. (They _had noticed_ that I am weak.)
Past Perfect Continuous	_Gin_talupangod _pa_	_Gintalupangod pa_ nila nga maluya ako. (They _had been noticing_ that I am weak.)
Present Simple	_Na_talupangdan	_Natalupangdan_ nila nga maluya ako. (They _notice_ that I am weak.)
Present Continuous	_Gina_talupangod	_Ginatalupangod_ nila nga maluya ako. (They _are noticing_ that I am weak.)
Present Perfect Simple	_Na_talupangdan _na_	_Natalupangdan na_ nila nga maluya ako. (They _have noticed_ that I am weak.)
Present Perfect Continuous	_Gina_talupangod _pa_	_Ginatalupangod pa_ nila nga maluya ako. (They _have been noticing_ that I am weak.)
Future Simple	_Ma_talupangdan	_Matalupangdan_ nila nga maluya ako. (They _will notice_ that I am weak.)
Future Continuous	_Paga_talupangdon	_Pagatalupangdon_ nila nga maluya ako. (They _will be noticing_ that I am weak.)
Future Perfect Simple	_Ma_talupangdan _na_	_Matalupangdan na_ kuntani nila nga maluya ako. (They _will have noticed_ that I am weak by then.)

Future Perfect Continuous	*Paga*talupangdon *pa*	*Pagatalupangdon pa* nila nga maluya ako. (They *will have been noticing* that I am weak.)

63. To open: buksan

Tenses	Word	Examples
Past Simple	**Gin**buksan	*Ginbuksan* niya ang lata. (He *opened* the can.)
Past Continuous	**Gin**buksan	*Ginbuksan* niya ang lata. (He *was opening* the can.)
Past Perfect Simple	**Gin**buksan **na**	*Ginbuksan na* niya ang lata. (He *had opened* the can.)
Past Perfect Continuous	**Gin**buksan **pa**	*Ginbuksan pa* niya ang lata. (He *had been opening* the can.)
Present Simple	**Gina**buksan	*Ginabuksan* niya ang lata. (He *opens* the can.)
Present Continuous	**Gina**buksan	*Ginabuksan* niya ang lata. (He *is opening* the can.)
Present Perfect Simple	**Na**buksan **na**	*Nabuksan na* niya ang lata. (He *has opened* the can.)
Present Perfect Continuous	**Gina**buksan **pa**	*Ginabuksan pa* niya ang lata. (He *has been opening* the can.)
Future Simple	**Paga**buksan	*Pagabuksan* niya ang lata. (He *will open* the can.)
Future Continuous	**Paga**buksan	*Pagabuksan* niya ang lata. (He *will be opening* the can.)
Future Perfect Simple	**Paga**buksan **na**	*Pagabuksan na* kuntani niya ang lata. (He *will have opened* the can by then.)
Future Perfect Continuous	**Paga**buksan **pa**	*Pagabuksan pa* niya ang lata. (He *will have been opening* the can.)

64. To play: hampang

Tenses	Word	Examples
Past Simple	_Nag_hampang	_Naghampang_ ang mga bata sa gua. (The children _played_ outside.)
Past Continuous	_Nag_hampang	_Naghampang_ ang mga bata sa gua. (The children _were playing_ outside.)
Past Perfect Simple	_Nag_hampang _na_	_Naghampang na_ ang mga bata sa gua. (The children _had played_ outside.)
Past Perfect Continuous	_Nag_hampang _pa_	_Naghampang pa_ ang mga bata sa gua. (The children _had been playing_ outside.)
Present Simple	_Naga_hampang	_Nagahampang_ ang mga bata sa gua. (The children _play_ outside.)
Present Continuous	_Naga_hampang	_Nagahampang_ ang mga bata sa gua. (The children _are playing_ outside.)
Present Perfect Simple	_Naga_hampang _na_	_Nagahampang na_ ang mga bata sa gua. (The children _have played_ outside.)
Present Perfect Continuous	_Naga_hampang _pa_	_Nagahampang pa_ ang mga bata sa gua. (The children _have been playing_ outside.)
Future Simple	_Maga_hampang	_Magahampang_ ang mga bata sa gua. (The children _will play_ outside.)
Future Continuous	_Maga_hampang	_Magahampang_ ang mga bata sa gua. (The children _will be playing_ outside.)
Future Perfect Simple	_Maga_hampang _na_	_Magahampang na_ kuntani ang mga bata sa gua. (The children _will have played_ outside by then.)
Future Perfect Continuous	_Maga_hampang _pa_	_Magahampang pa_ ang mga bata sa gua. (The children _will have been playing_ outside.)

65. To put: butang

Tenses	Word	Examples
Past Simple	*Nag*butang	*Nagbutang* sila sang pagkaon sa lamesa. (They *put* food on the table.)
Past Continuous	*Nag*butang	*Nagbutang* sila sang pagkaon sa lamesa. (They *were putting* food on the table.)
Past Perfect Simple	*Nag*butang *na*	*Nagbutang na* sila sang pagkaon sa lamesa. (They *had put* food on the table.)
Past Perfect Continuous	*Nag*butang *pa*	*Nagbutang pa* sila sang pagkaon sa lamesa. (They *had been putting* food on the table.)
Present Simple	*Naga*butang	*Nagabutang* sila sang pagkaon sa lamesa. (They *put* food on the table.)
Present Continuous	*Naga*butang	*Nagabutang* sila sang pagkaon sa lamesa. (They *are putting* food on the table.)
Present Perfect Simple	*Naga*butang *na*	*Nagabutang na* sila sang pagkaon sa lamesa. (They *have put* food on the table.)
Present Perfect Continuous	*Naga*butang *pa*	*Nagabutang pa* sila sang pagkaon sa lamesa. (They *have been putting* food on the table.)
Future Simple	*Maga*butang	*Magabutang* sila sang pagkaon sa lamesa. (They *will put* food on the table.)
Future Continuous	*Maga*butang	*Magabutang* sila sang pagkaon sa lamesa. (They *will be putting* food on the table.)
Future Perfect Simple	*Maga*butang *na*	*Magabutang na* kuntani sila sang pagkaon sa lamesa. (They *will have put* food on the table by then.)

Future Perfect Continuous	*Maga*butang *pa*	*Magabutang pa* sila sang pagkaon sa lamesa. (They *will have been putting* food on the table.)

66. To read: basa

Tenses	Word	Examples
Past Simple	*Nag*basa	*Nagbasa* ako sang pamantalaan. (I *read* the newspaper.)
Past Continuous	*Nag*basa	*Nagbasa* ako sang pamantalaan. (I *was reading* the newspaper.)
Past Perfect Simple	*Nag*basa *na*	*Nagbasa na* ako sang pamantalaan. (I *had read* the newspaper.)
Past Perfect Continuous	*Nag*basa *pa*	*Nagbasa pa* ako sang pamantalaan. (I *had been reading* the newspaper.)
Present Simple	*Naga*basa	*Nagabasa* ako sang pamantalaan. (I *read* the newspaper.)
Present Continuous	*Naga*basa	*Nagabasa* ako sang pamantalaan. (I *am reading* the newspaper.)
Present Perfect Simple	*Naga*basa *na*	*Nagabasa na* ako sang pamantalaan. (I *have read* the newspaper.)
Present Perfect Continuous	*Naga*basa *pa*	*Nagabasa pa* ako sang pamantalaan. (I *have been reading* the newspaper.)
Future Simple	*Maga*basa	*Magabasa* ako sang pamantalaan. (I *will read* the newspaper.)
Future Continuous	*Maga*basa	*Magabasa* ako sang pamantalaan. (I *will be reading* the newspaper.)
Future Perfect Simple	*Maga*basa *na*	*Magabasa na* kuntani ako sang pamantalaan. (I *will have read* the newspaper by then.)
Future Perfect Continuous	*Maga*basa *pa*	*Magabasa pa* ako sang pamantalaan. (I *will have been reading* the newspaper.)

67. To receive: baton

Tenses	Word	Examples
Past Simple	*Gin*baton	*Ginbaton* niya ang regalo. (He *received* the gift.)
Past Continuous	*Gin*baton	*Ginbaton* niya ang regalo. (He *was receiving* the gift.)
Past Perfect Simple	*Gin*baton *na*	*Ginbaton na* niya ang regalo. (He *had received* the gift.)
Past Perfect Continuous	*Gin*baton *pa*	*Ginbaton pa* niya ang regalo. (He *had been receiving* the gift.)
Present Simple	*Gina*baton	*Ginabaton* niya ang regalo. (He *receives* the gift.)
Present Continuous	*Gina*baton	*Ginabaton* niya ang regalo. (He *is receiving* the gift.)
Present Perfect Simple	*Gina*baton *na*	*Ginabaton na* niya ang regalo. (He *has received* the gift.)
Present Perfect Continuous	*Gina*baton *pa*	*Ginabaton pa* niya ang regalo. (He *has been receiving* the gift.)
Future Simple	*Maga*baton	*Magabaton* sia sang regalo. (He *will receive* the gift.)
Future Continuous	*Maga*baton	*Magabaton* sia sang regalo. (He *will be receiveing* the gift.)
Future Perfect Simple	*Maga*baton *na*	*Magabaton na* kuntani sia sang regalo. (He *will have received* the gift by then.)
Future Perfect Continuous	*Maga*baton *pa*	*Magabaton pa* sia sang regalo. (He *will have been receiving* the gift.)

68. To remember: dumdom

Tenses	Word	Examples
Past Simple	*Gin*dumdom	*Gindumdom* ko ang akon obligasyon. (I *remembered* my obligation.)
Past Continuous	*Gin*dumdom	*Gindumdom* ko ang akon obligasyon. (I *was remembering* my obligation.)
Past Perfect Simple	*Gin*dumdom *na*	*Gindumdom na* nakon ang akon obligasyon. (I *had remembered* my obligation.)
Past Perfect Continuous	*Gin*dumdom *pa*	*Gindumdom pa* nakon ang akon obligasyon. (I *had been remembering* my obligation.)
Present Simple	*Gina*dumdom	*Ginadumdom* ko ang akon obligasyon. (I *remember* my obligation.)
Present Continuous	*Gina*dumdom	*Ginadumdom* ko ang akon obligasyon. (I *am remembering* my obligation.)
Present Perfect Simple	*Gina*dumdom *na*	*Ginadumdom na* nakon ang akon obligasyon. (I *have remembered* my obligation.)
Present Perfect Continuous	*Gina*dumdom *pa*	*Ginadumdom pa* nakon ang akon obligasyon. (I *have been remembering* my obligation.)
Future Simple	*Maga*dumdom	*Magadumdom* ako sang akon obligasyon. (I *will remember* my obligation.)
Future Continuous	*Maga*dumdom	*Magadumdom* ako sang akon obligasyon. (I *will be remembering* my obligation.)
Future Perfect Simple	*Maga*dumdom *na*	*Magadumdom na* kuntani ako sang akon obligasyon. (I *will have remembered* my obligation by then.)

Future Perfect Continuous	*Maga*dumdom *pa*	*Magadumdom pa* ako sang akon obligasyon. (I *will have been remembering* my obligation.)

69. To repeat: sulit

Tenses	Word	Examples
Past Simple	**Gin**sulit	*Ginsulit* ko ang iya obra. (I *repeated* his work.)
Past Continuous	**Gin**sulit	*Ginsulit* ko ang iya obra. (I *was repeating* his work.)
Past Perfect Simple	**Gin**sulit **na**	*Ginsulit na* nakon ang iya obra. (I *had repeated* his work.)
Past Perfect Continuous	**Gin**sulit **pa**	*Ginsulit pa* nakon ang iya obra. (I *had been repeating* his work.)
Present Simple	**Gina**sulit	*Ginasulit* ko ang iya obra. (I *repeat* his work.)
Present Continuous	**Gina**sulit	*Ginasulit* ko ang iya obra. (I *am repeating* his work.)
Present Perfect Simple	**Gina**sulit **na**	*Ginasulit na* nakon ang iya obra. (I *have repeated* his work.)
Present Perfect Continuous	**Gina**sulit **pa**	*Ginasulit pa* nakon ang iya obra. (I *have been repeating* his work.)
Future Simple	**Maga**sulit	*Magasulit* ako sang iya obra. (I *will repeat* his work.)
Future Continuous	**Maga**sulit	*Magasulit* ako sang iya obra. (I *will be repeating* his work.)
Future Perfect Simple	**Maga**sulit **na**	*Magasulit na* kuntani ako sang iya obra. (I *will have repeated* his work by then.)
Future Perfect Continuous	**Maga**sulit **pa**	*Magasulit pa* ako sang iya obra. (I *will have been repeating* his work.)

70. To return: balik

Tenses	Word	Examples
Past Simple	*Nag*balik	*Nagbalik* ang mga tawo sa ila balay. (People *returned* to their home.)
Past Continuous	*Nag*balik	*Nagbalik* ang mga tawo sa ila balay. (People *were returning* to their home.)
Past Perfect Simple	*Nag*balik *na*	*Nagbalik na* ang mga tawo sa ila balay. (People *had returned* to their home.)
Past Perfect Continuous	*Nag*balik *pa*	*Nagbalik pa* ang mga tawo sa ila balay. (People *had been returning* to their home.)
Present Simple	*Naga*balik	*Nagabalik* ang mga tawo sa ila balay. (People *return* to their home.)
Present Continuous	*Naga*balik	*Nagabalik* ang mga tawo sa ila balay. (People *are returning* to their home.)
Present Perfect Simple	*Naga*balik *na*	*Nagabalik na* ang mga tawo sa ila balay. (People *have returned* to their home.)
Present Perfect Continuous	*Naga*balik *pa*	*Nagabalik pa* ang mga tawo sa ila balay. (People *have been returning* to their home.)
Future Simple	*Maga*balik	*Magabalik* ang mga tawo sa ila balay. (People *will return* to their home.)
Future Continuous	*Maga*balik	*Magabalik* ang mga tawo sa ila balay. (People *will be returning* to their home.)
Future Perfect Simple	*Maga*balik *na*	*Magabalik na* kuntani ang mga tawo sa ila balay. (People *will have been returned* to their home by then.)
Future Perfect Continuous	*Maga*balik *pa*	*Magabalik pa* ang mga tawo sa ila balay. (People *will have been returning* to their home.)

71. To run: dalagan

Tenses	Word	Examples
Past Simple	*Nag*dalagan	*Nagdalagan* si Antonia para sugataon sila. (Antonia *ran* to meet them.)
Past Continuous	*Nag*dalagan	*Nagdalagan* si Antonia para sugataon sila. (Antonia *was running* to meet them.)
Past Perfect Simple	*Nag*dalagan *na*	*Nagdalagan na* si Antonia para sugataon sila. (Antonia *had ran* to meet them.)
Past Perfect Continuous	*Nag*dalagan *pa*	*Nagdalagan pa* si Antonia para sugataon sila. (Antonia *had been running* to meet them.)
Present Simple	*Naga*dalagan	*Nagadalagan* si Antonia para sugataon sila. (Antonia *runs* to meet them.)
Present Continuous	*Naga*dalagan	*Nagadalagan* si Antonia para sugataon sila. (Antonia *is running* to meet them.)
Present Perfect Simple	*Naga*dalagan *na*	*Nagadalagan na* si Antonia para sugataon sila. (Antonia *has ran* to meet them.)
Present Perfect Continuous	*Naga*dalagan	*Nagadalagan pa* si Antonia para sugataon sila. (Antonia *has been running* to meet them.)
Future Simple	*Maga*dalagan	*Magadalagan* si Antonia para sugataon sila. (Antonia *will run* to meet them.)
Future Continuous	*Maga*dalagan	*Magadalagan* si Antonia para sugataon sila. (Antonia *will be running* to meet them.)
Future Perfect Simple	*Maga*dalagan *na*	*Magadalagan na* kuntani si Antonia para sugataon sila. (Antonia *will have run* to meet them by then.)

Future Perfect Continuous	_**Maga**dalagan **pa**_	_Magadalagan pa_ si Antonia para sugataon sila. (Antonia _will have been running_ to meet them.)

72. To say: siling

Tenses	Word	Examples
Past Simple	*Nag*siling	*Nagsiling* sia sang kamatuoran. (She *said* the truth.)
Past Continuous	*Nag*siling	*Nagsiling* sia sang kamatuoran. (She *was saying* the truth.)
Past Perfect Simple	*Nag*siling *na*	*Nagsiling na* sia sang kamatuoran. (She *had said* the truth.)
Past Perfect Continuous	*Nag*siling *pa*	*Nagsiling pa* sia sang kamatuoran. (She *had been saying* the truth.)
Present Simple	*Naga*siling	*Nagasiling* sia sang kamatuoran. (She *says* the truth.)
Present Continuous	*Naga*siling	*Nagasiling* sia sang kamatuoran. (She *is saying* the truth.)
Present Perfect Simple	*Naga*siling *na*	*Nagasiling na* sia sang kamatuoran. (She *has said* the truth.)
Present Perfect Continuous	*Naga*siling *pa*	*Nagasiling pa* sia sang kamatuoran. (She *has been saying* the truth.)
Future Simple	*Maga*siling	*Magasiling* sia sang kamatuoran. (She *will say* the truth.)
Future Continuous	*Maga*siling	*Magasiling* sia sang kamatuoran. (She *will be saying* the truth.)
Future Perfect Simple	*Maga*siling *na*	*Magasiling na* kuntani sia sang kamatuoran. (She *will have said* the truth by then.)
Future Perfect Continuous	*Maga*siling *pa*	*Magasiling pa* sia sang kamatuoran. (She *will have been saying* the truth.)

73. To scream: singgit

Tenses	Word	Examples
Past Simple	*Nag*singgit	*Nagsinggit* sia sing mabaskog. (She *screamed* aloud.)
Past Continuous	*Nag*singgit	*Nagsinggit* sia sing mabaskog. (She *was screaming* aloud.)
Past Perfect Simple	*Nag*singgit *na*	*Nagsinggit na* sia sing mabaskog. (She *had screamed* aloud.)
Past Perfect Continuous	*Nag*singgit *pa*	*Nagsinggit pa* sia sing mabaskog. (She *had been screaming* aloud.)
Present Simple	*Naga*singgit	*Nagasinggit* sia sing mabaskog. (She *screams* aloud.)
Present Continuous	*Naga*singgit	*Nagasinggit* sia sing mabaskog. (She *is screaming* aloud.)
Present Perfect Simple	*Naga*singgit *na*	*Nagasinggit na* sia sing mabaskog. (She *has screamed* aloud.)
Present Perfect Continuous	*Naga*singgit *pa*	*Nagasinggit pa* sia sing mabaskog. (She *has been screaming* aloud.)
Future Simple	*Maga*singgit	*Magasinggit* sia sing mabaskog. (She *will scream* aloud.)
Future Continuous	*Maga*singgit	*Magasinggit* sia sing mabaskog. (She *will be screaming* aloud.)
Future Perfect Simple	*Maga*singgit *na*	*Magasinggit na* kuntani sia sing mabaskog. (She *will have screamed* aloud by then.)
Future Perfect Continuous	*Maga*singgit *pa*	*Magasinggit pa* sia sing mabaskog. (She *will have been screaming* aloud.)

74. To see: kita

Tenses	Word	Examples
Past Simple	*Na*kita	*Nakita* ko ini sa Internet. (I *saw* it in the Internet.)
Past Continuous	*Na*kita	*Nakita* ko ini sa Internet. (I *was seeing* it in the Internet.)
Past Perfect Simple	*Na*kita *na*	*Nakita na* nakon ini sa Internet. (I *had seen* it in the Internet.)
Past Perfect Continuous	*Na*kita *pa*	*Nakita pa* nakon ini sa Internet. (I *had been seeing* it in the Internet.)
Present Simple	*Na*kita	*Nakita* ko ini sa Internet. (I *see* it in the Internet.)
Present Continuous	*Na*kita	*Nakita* ko ini sa Internet. (I *am seeing* it in the Internet.)
Present Perfect Simple	*Na*kita *na*	*Nakita na* nakon ini sa Internet. (I *have seen* it in the Internet.)
Present Perfect Continuous	*Na*kita *pa*	*Nakita pa* nakon ini sa Internet. (I *have been seeing* it in the Internet.)
Future Simple	*Ma*kita	*Makita* ko ini sa Internet. (I *will see* it in the Internet.)
Future Continuous	*Ma*kita	*Makita* ko ini sa Internet. (I *will be seeing* it in the Internet.)
Future Perfect Simple	*Ma*kita *na*	*Makita na* kuntani nakon ini sa Internet. (I *will have seen* it in the Internet by then.)
Future Perfect Continuous	*Ma*kita *pa*	*Makita pa* nakon ini sa Internet. (I *will have been seeing* it in the Internet.)

75. To seem: daw

Tenses	Word	Examples
Past Simple	*Daw*	*Daw* malipayon si Glenda sini nga mga inadlaw. (Glenda *seemed* happy these days.)
Past Continuous	No equivalent	No equivalent
Past Perfect Simple	*Daw*	*Daw* malipayon si Glenda sini nga mga inadlaw. (Glenda *had seemed* happythese days.)
Past Perfect Continuous		No equivalent
Present Simple	*Daw*	*Daw* malipayon si Glenda sini nga mga inadlaw. (Glenda *seems* happy these days.)
Present Continuous		No equivalent
Present Perfect Simple	*Daw*	*Daw* malipayon si Glenda sini nga mga inadlaw. (Glenda *has seemed* happy these days.)
Present Perfect Continuous	No equivalent	No equivalent
Future Simple	No equivalent	No equivalent
Future Continuous	No equivalent	No equivalent
Future Perfect Simple	No equivalent	No equivalent
Future Perfect Continuous	No equivalent	No equivalent

76. To sell: baligya

Tenses	Word	Examples
Past Simple	*Nag*baligya	*Nagbaligya* sila sang mga bulak. (They *sold* flowers.)
Past Continuous	*Nag*baligya	*Nagbaligya* sila sang mga bulak. (They *were selling* flowers.)
Past Perfect Simple	*Nag*baligya *na*	*Nagbaligya na* sila sang mga bulak. (They *had sold* flowers.)
Past Perfect Continuous	*Nag*baligya *pa*	*Nagbaligya pa* sila sang mga bulak. (They *had been selling* flowers.)
Present Simple	*Naga*baligya	*Nagabaligya* sila sang mga bulak. (They *sell* flowers.)
Present Continuous	*Naga*baligya	*Nagabaligya* sila sang mga bulak. (They *are selling* flowers.)
Present Perfect Simple	*Naga*baligya *na*	*Nagabaligya na* sila sang mga bulak. (They *have sold* flowers.)
Present Perfect Continuous	*Naga*baligya *pa*	*Nagabaligya pa* sila sang mga bulak. (They *have been selling* flowers.)
Future Simple	*Maga*baligya	*Magabaligya* sila sang mga bulak. (They *will sell* flowers.)
Future Continuous	*Maga*baligya	*Magabaligya* sila sang mga bulak. (They *will be selling* flowers.)
Future Perfect Simple	*Maga*baligya *na*	*Magabaligya na* kuntani sila sang mga bulak. (They *will have sold* flowers by then.)
Future Perfect Continuous	*Maga*baligya *pa*	*Magabaligya pa* sila sang mga bulak. (They *will have been selling* flowers.)

77. To send: padala

Tenses	Word	Examples
Past Simple	*Nag*padala	*Nagpadala* sila sang ila panamyaw. (They *sent* their greetings.)
Past Continuous	*Nag*padala	*Nagpadala* sila sang ila panamyaw. (They *were sending* their greetings.)
Past Perfect Simple	*Nag*padala *na*	*Nagpadala na* sila sang ila panamyaw. (They *had sent* their greetings.)
Past Perfect Continuous	*Nag*padala *pa*	*Nagpadala pa* sila sang ila panamyaw. (They *had been sending* their greetings.)
Present Simple	*Naga*padala	*Nagapadala* sila sang ila panamyaw. (They *send* their greetings.)
Present Continuous	*Naga*padala	*Nagapadala* sila sang ila panamyaw. (They *are sending* their greetings.)
Present Perfect Simple	*Naga*padala *na*	*Nagapadala na* sila sang ila panamyaw. (They *have sent* their greetings.)
Present Perfect Continuous	*Naga*padala *pa*	*Nagapadala pa* sila sang ila panamyaw. (They *have been sending* their greetings.)
Future Simple	*Maga*padala	*Magapadala* sila sang ila panamyaw. (They *will send* their greetings.)
Future Continuous	*Maga*padala	*Magapadala* sila sang ila panamyaw. (They *will be sending* their greetings.)
Future Perfect Simple	*Maga*padala *na*	*Magapadala na* kuntani sila sang ila panamyaw. (They *will have sent* their greetings by then.)
Future Perfect Continuous	*Maga*padala *pa*	*Magapadala pa* sila sang ila panamyaw. (They *will have been sending* their greetings.)

78. To show: pakita

Tenses	Word	Examples
Past Simple	**Nag**pakita	*Nagpakita* sia sang maayo nga halimbawa. (He *showed* a good example.)
Past Continuous	**Nag**pakita	*Nagapakita* sia sang maayo nga halimbawa. (He *was showing* a good example.)
Past Perfect Simple	**Nag**pakita **na**	*Nagpakita na* sia sang maayo nga halimbawa. (He *had shown* a good example.)
Past Perfect Continuous	**Nag**pakita **pa**	*Nagpakita pa* sia sang maayo nga halimbawa. (He *had been showing* a good example.)
Present Simple	**Naga**pakita	*Nagapakita* sia sang maayo nga halimbawa. (He *shows* a good example.)
Present Continuous	**Naga**pakita	*Nagapakita* sia sang maayo nga halimbawa. (He *is showing* a good example.)
Present Perfect Simple	**Naga**pakita **na**	*Nagapakita na* sia sang maayo nga halimbawa. (He *has shown* a good example.)
Present Perfect Continuous	**Naga**pakita **pa**	*Nagapakita pa* sia sang maayo nga halimbawa. (He *has been showing* a good example.)
Future Simple	**Maga**pakita	*Magapakita* sia sang maayo nga halimbawa. (He *will show* a good example.)
Future Continuous	**Maga**pakita	*Magapakita* sia sang maayo nga halimbawa. (He *will be showing* a good example.)

Future Perfect Simple	_Maga_pakita _na_	_Magapakita na_ kuntani sia sang maayo nga halimbawa. (He _will have shown_ a good example by then.)
Future Perfect Continuous	_Maga_pakita _pa_	_Magapakita pa_ sia sang maayo nga halimbawa. (He _will have been showing_ a good example.)

79. To sing: kanta

Tenses	Word	Examples
Past Simple	_Nag_kanta	_Nagkanta_ sila sang mabaskog. (They _sang_ aloud.)
Past Continuous	_Nag_kanta	_Nagkanta_ sila sang mabaskog. (They _were singing_ aloud.)
Past Perfect Simple	_Nag_kanta _na_	_Nagkanta na_ sila sang mabaskog. (They _had sang_ aloud.)
Past Perfect Continuous	_Nag_kanta _pa_	_Nagkanta pa_ sila sang mabaskog. (They _had been singing_ aloud.)
Present Simple	_Naga_kanta	_Nagakanta_ sila sang mabaskog. (They _sing_ aloud.)
Present Continuous	_Naga_kanta	_Nagakanta_ sila sang mabaskog. (They _are singing_ aloud.)
Present Perfect Simple	_Naga_kanta _na_	_Nagakanta na_ sila sang mabaskog. (They _have sang_ aloud.)
Present Perfect Continuous	_Naga_kanta _pa_	_Nagakanta pa_ sila sang mabaskog. (They _have been singing_ aloud.)
Future Simple	_Maga_kanta	_Magakanta_ sila sang mabaskog. (They _will sing_ aloud.)
Future Continuous	_Maga_kanta	_Magakanta_ sila sang mabaskog. (They _will be singing_ aloud.)
Future Perfect Simple	_Maga_kanta _na_	_Magakanta na_ kuntani sila sang mabaskog. (They _will have sung_ aloud by then.)
Future Perfect Continuous	_Maga_kanta _pa_	_Magakanta pa_ sila sang mabaskog. (They _will have been singing_ aloud.)

80. To sit down: pungko

Tenses	Word	Examples
Past Simple	*Nag*pungko	*Nagpungko* sia sa atubangan. (He *sat* in front.)
Past Continuous	*Nag*pungko	*Nagpungko* sia sa atubangan. (He *was sitting* in front.)
Past Perfect Simple	*Nag*pungko *na*	*Nagpungko na* sia sa atubangan. (He *had sat* in front.)
Past Perfect Continuous	*Nag*pungko *pa*	*Nagpungko pa* sia sa atubangan. (He *had been sitting* in front.)
Present Simple	*Naga*pungko	*Nagapungko* sia sa atubangan. (He *sits* in front.)
Present Continuous	*Naga*pungko	*Nagapungko* sia sa atubangan. (He *is sitting* in front.)
Present Perfect Simple	*Naga*pungko *na*	*Nagapungko na* sia sa atubangan. (He *has sat* in front.)
Present Perfect Continuous	*Naga*pungko *pa*	*Nagapungko pa* sia sa atubangan. (He *has been sitting* in front.)
Future Simple	*Maga*pungko	*Magapungko* sia sa atubangan. (He *will sit* in front.)
Future Continuous	*Maga*pungko	*Magapungko* sia sa atubangan. (He *will be sitting* in front.)
Future Perfect Simple	*Maga*pungko *na*	*Magapungko na* kuntani sia sa atubangan. (He *will have sat* in front by then.)
Future Perfect Continuous	*Maga*pungko *pa*	*Magapungko pa* sia sa atubangan. (He *will have been sitting* in front.)

81. To sleep: tulog

Tenses	Word	Examples
Past Simple	*Nag*tulog	*Nagtulog* ang mga bata. (The children *slept*.)
Past Continuous	*Nag*tulog	*Nagtulog* ang mga bata. (The children *was sleeping*.)
Past Perfect Simple	*Nag*tulog *na*	*Nagtulog na* ang mga bata. (The children *had slept*.)
Past Perfect Continuous	*Nag*tulog *pa*	*Nagtulog pa* ang mga bata. (The children *had been sleeping*.)
Present Simple	*Naga*tulog	*Nagatulog* ang mga bata. (The children *sleep*.)
Present Continuous	*Naga*tulog	*Nagatulog* ang mga bata. (The children *are sleeping*.)
Present Perfect Simple	*Naga*tulog *na*	*Nagatulog na* ang mga bata. (The children *has slept*.)
Present Perfect Continuous	*Naga*tulog *pa*	*Nagatulog pa* ang mga bata. (The children *has been sleeping*.)
Future Simple	*Maga*tulog	*Magatulog* ang mga bata. (The children *will sleep*.)
Future Continuous	*Maga*tulog	*Magatulog* ang mga bata. (The children *will be sleeping*.)
Future Perfect Simple	*Maga*tulog *na*	*Magatulog na* kuntani ang mga bata. (The children *will have slept* by then.)
Future Perfect Continuous	*Maga*tulog *pa*	*Magatulog pa* ang mga bata. (The children *will have been sleeping*.)

82. To smile: yuhom

Tenses	Word	Examples
Past Simple	*Nag*yuhom	*Nagyuhom* sia sa akon. (She *smiled* at me.)
Past Continuous	*Nag*yuhom	*Nagyuhom* sia sa akon. (She *was smiling* at me.)
Past Perfect Simple	*Nag*yuhom *na*	*Nagyuhom na* sia sa akon. (She *had smiled* at me.)
Past Perfect Continuous	*Nag*yuhom *pa*	*Nagyuhom pa* sia sa akon. (She *had been smiling* at me.)
Present Simple	*Naga*yuhom	*Nagayuhom* sia sa akon. (She *smiles* at me.)
Present Continuous	*Naga*yuhom	*Nagayuhom* sia sa akon. (She *is smiling* at me.)
Present Perfect Simple	*Naga*yuhom *na*	*Nagayuhom na* sia sa akon. (She *has smiled* at me.)
Present Perfect Continuous	*Naga*yuhom *pa*	*Nagayuhom pa* sia sa akon. (She *has been smiling* at me.)
Future Simple	*Maga*yuhom	*Magayuhom* sia sa akon. (She *will smile* at me.)
Future Continuous	*Maga*yuhom	*Magayuhom* sia sa akon. (She *will be smiling* at me.)
Future Perfect Simple	*Maga*yuhom *na*	*Magayuhom na* kuntani sia sa akon. (She *will have smiled* at me by then.)
Future Perfect Continuous	*Maga*yuhom *pa*	*Magayuhom pa* sia sa akon. (She *will have been smiling* at me.)

83. To speak: hambal

Tenses	Word	Examples
Past Simple	*Nag*hambal	*Naghambal* sia sing kalmado. (He *spoke* calmly.)
Past Continuous	*Nag*hambal	*Naghambal* sia sing kalmado. (He *was speaking* calmly.)
Past Perfect Simple	*Nag*hambal *na*	*Naghambal na* sia sing kalmado. (He *had spoke* calmly.)
Past Perfect Continuous	*Nag*hambal *pa*	*Naghambal pa* sia sing kalmado. (He *had been speaking* calmly.)
Present Simple	*Naga*hambal	*Nagahambal* sia sing kalmado. (He *speaks* calmly.)
Present Continuous	*Naga*hambal	*Nagahambal* sia sing kalmado. (He *is speaking* calmly.)
Present Perfect Simple	*Naga*hambal *na*	*Nagahambal na* sia sing kalmado. (He *has smiled* calmly.)
Present Perfect Continuous	*Naga*hambal *pa*	*Nagahambal pa* sia sing kalmado. (He *has been speaking* calmly.)
Future Simple	*Maga*hambal	*Magahambal* sia sing kalmado. (He *will speak* calmly.)
Future Continuous	*Maga*hambal	*Magahambal* sia sing kalmado. (He *will be speaking* calmly.)
Future Perfect Simple	*Maga*hambal *na*	*Magahambal na* kuntani sia sing kalmado. (He *will have spoken* calmly by then.)
Future Perfect Continuous	*Maga*hambal *pa*	*Magahambal pa* sia sing kalmado. (He *will have been speaking* calmly.)

84. To stand: tindog

Tenses	Word	Examples
Past Simple	*Nag*tindog	*Nagtindog* sia sing tiso. (He *stood* straight.)
Past Continuous	*Nag*tindog	*Nagtindog* sia sing tiso. (He *was standing* straight.)
Past Perfect Simple	*Nag*tindog *na*	*Nagtindog na* sia sing tiso. (He *had stood* straight.)
Past Perfect Continuous	*Nag*tindog *pa*	*Nagtindog pa* sia sing tiso. (He *had been standing* straight.)
Present Simple	*Naga*tindog	*Nagatindog* sia sing tiso. (He *stands* straight.)
Present Continuous	*Naga*tindog	*Nagatindog* sia sing tiso. (He *is standing* straight.)
Present Perfect Simple	*Naga*tindog *na*	*Nagatindog na* sia sing tiso. (He *has stood* straight.)
Present Perfect Continuous	*Naga*tindog *pa*	*Nagatindog pa* sia sing tiso. (He *has been standing* straight.)
Future Simple	*Maga*tindog	*Magatindog* sia sing tiso. (He *will stand* straight.)
Future Continuous	*Maga*tindog	*Magatindog* sia sing tiso. (He *will be standing* straight.)
Future Perfect Simple	*Maga*tindog *na*	*Magatindog na* kuntani sia sing tiso. (He *will have stood* straight by then.)
Future Perfect Continuous	*Maga*tindog *pa*	*Magatindog pa* sia sing tiso. (He *will have been standing* straight.)

91

85. To start: sugod

Tenses	Word	Examples
Past Simple	*Nag*sugod	*Nagsugod* sila obra aga pa. (They *started* working early.)
Past Continuous	*Nag*sugod	*Nagsugod* sila obra aga pa. (They *were starting* working early.)
Past Perfect Simple	*Nag*sugod *na*	*Nagsugod na* sila obra aga pa. (They *had started* working early.)
Past Perfect Continuous	*Nag*sugod *pa*	*Nagsugod pa* sila obra aga pa. (They *had been starting* working early.)
Present Simple	*Naga*sugod	*Nagasugod* sila obra aga pa. (They *start* working early.)
Present Continuous	*Naga*sugod	*Nagasugod* sila obra aga pa. (They *are starting* working early.)
Present Perfect Simple	*Naga*sugod *na*	*Nagasugod na* sila obra aga pa. (They *have started* working early.)
Present Perfect Continuous	*Naga*sugod *pa*	*Nagasugod pa* sila obra aga pa. (They *have been starting* working early.)
Future Simple	*Maga*sugod	*Magasugod* sila obra aga pa. (They *will start* working early.)
Future Continuous	*Maga*sugod	*Magasugod* sila obra aga pa. (They *will be starting* working early.)
Future Perfect Simple	*Maga*sugod *na*	*Magasugod na* kuntani sila obra aga pa. (They *will have started* working early by then.)
Future Perfect Continuous	*Maga*sugod *pa*	*Magasugod pa* sila obra aga pa. (They *will have been starting* working early.)

86. To stay: istar

Tenses	Word	Examples
Past Simple	*Nag*-istar	*Nag-istar* si Ben sa Pilipinas. (Ben *stayed* in the Philippines.)
Past Continuous	*Nag*-istar	*Nag-istar* si Ben sa Pilipinas. (Ben *was staying* in the Philippines.)
Past Perfect Simple	*Nag*-istar *na*	*Nag-istar na* si Ben sa Pilipinas. (Ben *had stayed* in the Philippines.)
Past Perfect Continuous	*Nag*-istar *pa*	*Nag-istar pa* si Ben sa Pilipinas. (Ben *had been staying* in the Philippines.)
Present Simple	*Naga*istar	*Nagaistar* si Ben sa Pilipinas. (Ben *stays* in the Philippines.)
Present Continuous	*Naga*istar	*Nagaistar* si Ben sa Pilipinas. (Ben *is staying* in the Philippines.)
Present Perfect Simple	*Naga*istar *na*	*Nagaistar na* si Ben sa Pilipinas. (Ben *has stayed* in the Philippines.)
Present Perfect Continuous	*Naga*istar *pa*	*Nagaistar pa* si Ben sa Pilipinas. (Ben *has been staying* in the Philippines.)
Future Simple	*Maga*istar	*Magaistar* si Ben sa Pilipinas. (Ben *will stay* in the Philippines.)
Future Continuous	*Maga*istar	*Magaistar* si Ben sa Pilipinas. (Ben *will be staying* in the Philippines.)
Future Perfect Simple	*Maga*istar *na*	*Magaistar na* kuntani si Ben sa Pilipinas. (Ben *will have stayed* in the Philippines by then.)
Future Perfect Continuous	*Maga*istar *pa*	*Magaistar pa* si Ben sa Pilipinas. (Ben *will have been staying* in the Philippines.)

87. To take: kuha

Tenses	Word	Examples
Past Simple	*Nag*kuha	*Nagkuha* ako sang medikal nga eksaminasyon. (I *took* medical examination.)
Past Continuous	*Nag*kuha	*Nagkuha* ako sang medikal nga eksaminasyon. (I *was taking* medical examination.)
Past Perfect Simple	*Nag*kuha *na*	*Nagkuha na* ako sang medikal nga eksaminasyon. (I *had taken* medical examination.)
Past Perfect Continuous	*Nag*kuha *pa*	*Nagkuha pa* ako sang medikal nga eksaminasyon. (I *had been taking* medical examination.)
Present Simple	*Naga*kuha	*Nagakuha* ako sang medikal nga eksaminasyon. (I *take* medical examination.)
Present Continuous	*Naga*kuha	*Nagakuha* ako sang medikal nga eksaminasyon. (I *am taking* medical examination.)
Present Perfect Simple	*Naga*kuha *na*	*Nagakuha na* ako sang medikal nga eksaminasyon. (I *have taken* medical examination.)
Present Perfect Continuous	*Naga*kuha *pa*	*Nagakuha pa* ako sang medikal nga eksaminasyon. (I *have been taking* medical examination.)
Future Simple	*Maga*kuha	*Magakuha* ako sang medikal nga eksaminasyon. (I *will take* medical examination.)
Future Continuous	*Maga*kuha	*Magakuha* ako sang medikal nga eksaminasyon. (I *will be taking* medical examination.)

Future Perfect Simple	*Maga*kuha *na*	*Magakuha na* kuntani ako sang medikal nga eksaminasyon. (I *will have taken* medical examination by then.)
Future Perfect Continuous	*Maga*kuha *pa*	*Magakuha pa* ako sang medikal nga eksaminasyon. (I *will have been taking* medical examination.)

88. To talk: istorya

Tenses	Word	Examples
Past Simple	*Nag*-istorya	*Nag-istorya* sia parte sa iya pamilya. (He *talked* about his family.)
Past Continuous	*Nag*-istorya	*Nag-istorya* sia parte sa iya pamilya. (He *was talking* about his family.)
Past Perfect Simple	*Nag*-istorya *na*	*Nag-istorya na* sia parte sa iya pamilya. (He *had talked* about his family.)
Past Perfect Continuous	*Nag*-istorya *pa*	*Nag-istorya pa* sia parte sa iya pamilya. (He *had been talking* about his family.)
Present Simple	*Naga*istorya	*Nagaistorya* sia parte sa iya pamilya. (He *talks* about his family.)
Present Continuous	*Naga*istorya	*Nagaistorya* sia parte sa iya pamilya. (He *is talking* about his family.)
Present Perfect Simple	*Naga*istorya *na*	*Nagaistorya na* sia parte sa iya pamilya. (He *has talked* about his family.)
Present Perfect Continuous	*Naga*istorya *pa*	*Nagaistorya pa* sia parte sa iya pamilya. (He *has been talking* about his family.)
Future Simple	*Maga*istorya	*Magaistorya* sia parte sa iya pamilya. (He *will talk* about his family.)
Future Continuous	*Maga*istorya	*Magaistorya* sia parte sa iya pamilya. (He *will be talking* about his family.)
Future Perfect Simple	*Maga*istorya *na*	*Magaistorya na* kuntani sia parte sa iya pamilya. (He *will have talked* about his family by then.)
Future Perfect Continuous	*Maga*istorya *pa*	*Magaistorya pa* sia parte sa iya pamilya. (He *will have been talking* about his family.)

89. To teach: tudlo

Tenses	Word	Examples
Past Simple	_Nag_tudlo	_Nagtudlo_ ako sa mga bata. (I _taught_ the children.)
Past Continuous	_Nag_tudlo	_Nagtudlo_ ako sa mga bata. (I _was teaching_ the children.)
Past Perfect Simple	_Nag_tudlo _na_	_Nagtudlo na_ ako sa mga bata. (I _had taught_ the children.)
Past Perfect Continuous	_Nag_tudlo _pa_	_Nagtudlo pa_ ako sa mga bata. (I _had been teaching_ the children.)
Present Simple	_Naga_tudlo	_Nagatudlo_ ako sa mga bata. (I _teach_ the children.)
Present Continuous	_Naga_tudlo	_Nagatudlo_ ako sa mga bata. (I _am teaching_ the children.)
Present Perfect Simple	_Naga_tudlo _na_	_Nagatudlo na_ ako sa mga bata. (I _have taught_ the children.)
Present Perfect Continuous	_Naga_tudlo _pa_	_Nagatudlo pa_ ako sa mga bata. (I _have been teaching_ the children.)
Future Simple	_Maga_tudlo	_Magatudlo_ ako sa mga bata. (I _will teach_ the children.)
Future Continuous	_Maga_tudlo	_Magatudlo_ ako sa mga bata. (I _will be teaching_ the children.)
Future Perfect Simple	_Maga_tudlo _na_	_Magatudlo na_ kuntani ako sa mga bata. (I _will have taught_ the children by then.)
Future Perfect Continuous	_Maga_tudlo _pa_	_Magatudlo pa_ ako sa mga bata. (I _will have been teaching_ the children.)

90. To think: hunahuna

Tenses	Word	Examples
Past Simple	*Nag*hunahuna	*Naghunahuna* sia parte sa espirituwal nga mga butang. (He *thought* about spiritual matters.)
Past Continuous	*Nag*hunahuna	*Naghunahuna* sia parte sa espirituwal nga mga butang. (He *was thinking* about spiritual matters.)
Past Perfect Simple	*Nag*hunahuna *na*	*Naghunahuna na* sia parte sa espirituwal nga mga butang. (He *had thought* about spiritual matters.)
Past Perfect Continuous	*Nag*hunahuna *pa*	*Naghunahuna pa* sia parte sa espirituwal nga mga butang. (He *had been thinking* about spiritual matters.)
Present Simple	*Naga*hunahuna	*Nagahunahuna* sia parte sa espirituwal nga mga butang. (He *thinks* about spiritual matters.)
Present Continuous	*Naga*hunahuna	*Nagahunahuna* sia parte sa espirituwal nga mga butang. (He *is thinking* about spiritual matters.)
Present Perfect Simple	*Naga*hunahuna *na*	*Nagahunahuna na* sia parte sa espirituwal nga mga butang. (He *has thought* about spiritual matters.)
Present Perfect Continuous	*Naga*hunahuna *pa*	*Nagahunahuna pa* sia parte sa espirituwal nga mga butang. (He *has been thinking* about spiritual matters.)
Future Simple	*Maga*hunahuna	*Magahunahuna* sia parte sa espirituwal nga mga butang. (He *will think* about spiritual matters.)
Future Continuous	*Maga*hunahuna	*Magahunahuna* sia parte sa espirituwal nga mga butang. (He *will be thinking* about spiritual matters.)

Future Perfect Simple	*Maga*hunahuna *na*	*Magahunahuna na* kuntani sia parte sa espirituwal nga mga butang. (He *will have thought* about spiritual matters by then.)
Future Perfect Continuous	*Maga*hunahuna *pa*	*Magahunahuna pa* sia parte sa espirituwal nga mga butang. (He *will have been thinking* about spiritual matters.)

91. To touch: tandog

Tenses	Word	Examples
Past Simple	_**Nag**tandog_	_Nagtandog_ sila sang mahigko nga mga butang. (They _touched_ unclean things.)
Past Continuous	_**Nag**tandog_	_Nagtandog_ sila sang mahigko nga mga butang. (They _were touching_ unclean things.)
Past Perfect Simple	_**Nag**tandog_ _**na**_	_Nagtandog na_ sila sang mahigko nga mga butang. (They _had touched_ unclean things.)
Past Perfect Continuous	_**Nag**tandog_ _**pa**_	_Nagtandog pa_ sila sang mahigko nga mga butang. (They _had been touching_ unclean things.)
Present Simple	_**Naga**tandog_	_Nagatandog_ sila sang mahigko nga mga butang. (They _touch_ unclean things.)
Present Continuous	_**Naga**tandog_	_Nagatandog_ sila sang mahigko nga mga butang. (They _are touching_ unclean things.)
Present Perfect Simple	_**Naga**tandog_ _**na**_	_Nagatandog na_ sila sang mahigko nga mga butang. (They _have touched_ unclean things.)
Present Perfect Continuous	_**Naga**tandog_ _**pa**_	_Nagatandog pa_ sila sang mahigko nga mga butang. (They _have been touching_ unclean things.)
Future Simple	_**Maga**tandog_	_Magatandog_ sila sang mahigko nga mga butang. (They _will touch_ unclean things.)
Future Continuous	_**Maga**tandog_	_Magatandog_ sila sang mahigko nga mga butang. (They _will be touching_ unclean things.)
Future Perfect Simple	_**Maga**tandog_ _**na**_	_Magatandog na_ kuntani sila sang mahigko nga mga butang. (They _will have touched_ unclean things by then.)

Future Perfect Continuous	*Maga*tandog *pa*	*Magatandog pa* sila sang mahigko nga mga butang. (They *will have been touching* unclean things.)

92. To travel: byahe

Tenses	Word	Examples
Past Simple	_**Nag**byahe_	_Nagbyahe_ sila sing ginatos ka milya. (They _traveled_ hundreds of miles.)
Past Continuous	_**Nag**byahe_	_Nagbyahe_ sila sing ginatos ka milya. (They _were traveling_ hundreds of miles.)
Past Perfect Simple	_**Nag**byahe_ _**na**_	_Nagbyahe na_ sila sing ginatos ka milya. (They _had traveled_ hundreds of miles.)
Past Perfect Continuous	_**Nag**byahe_ _**pa**_	_Nagbyahe pa_ sila sing ginatos ka milya. (They _had been traveling_ hundreds of miles.)
Present Simple	_**Naga**byahe_	_Nagabyahe_ sila sing ginatos ka milya. (They _travel_ hundreds of miles.)
Present Continuous	_**Naga**byahe_	_Nagabyahe_ sila sing ginatos ka milya. (They _are traveling_ hundreds of miles.)
Present Perfect Simple	_**Naga**byahe_ _**na**_	_Nagabyahe na_ sila sing ginatos ka milya. (They _have traveled_ hundreds of miles.)
Present Perfect Continuous	_**Naga**byahe_ _**pa**_	_Nagabyahe pa_ sila sing ginatos ka milya. (They _have been traveling_ hundreds of miles.)
Future Simple	_**Maga**byahe_	_Magabyahe_ sila sing ginatos ka milya. (They _will travel_ hundreds of miles.)
Future Continuous	_**Maga**byahe_	_Magabyahe_ sila sing ginatos ka milya. (They _will be traveling_ hundreds of miles.)
Future Perfect Simple	_**Maga**byahe_ _**na**_	_Magabyahe na_ kuntani sila sing ginatos ka milya. (They _will have traveled_ hundreds of miles by then.)
Future Perfect Continuous	_**Maga**byahe_ _**pa**_	_Magabyahe pa_ sila sing ginatos ka milya. (They _will have been traveling_ hundreds of miles.)

93. To understand: hangop, hangpan

Tenses	Word	Examples
Past Simple	*Na*hangpan	*Nahangpan* ko ang paathag. (I *understood* the explanation.)
Past Continuous	*Gin*hangop	*Ginhangop* ko ang paathag. (I *was understanding* the explanation.)
Past Perfect Simple	*Na*hangpan *na*	*Nahangpan na* nakon ang paathag. (I *had understood* the explanation.)
Past Perfect Continuous	*Gin*hangpan *pa*	*Ginhangop pa* nakon ang paathag. (I *had been understanding* the explanation.)
Present Simple	*Na*hangpan	*Nahangpan* ko ang paathag. (I *understand* the explanation.)
Present Continuous	*Gina*hangopn	*Ginahangop* ko ang paathag. (I *am understanding* the explanation.)
Present Perfect Simple	*Na*hangpan *na*	*Nahangpan na* nakon ang paathag. (I *have understood* the explanation.)
Present Perfect Continuous	*Gina*hangop *pa*	*Ginahangop pa* ko ang paathag. (I *have been understanding* the explanation.)
Future Simple	*Ma*hangpan	*Mahangpan* ko ang paathag. (I *will understand* the explanation.)
Future Continuous	*Ma*hangpan	*Mahangpan* ko ang paathag. (I *will be understanding* the explanation.)
Future Perfect Simple	*Ma*hangpan *na*	*Mahangpan na* kuntani nakon ang paathag. (I *will have understood* the explanation by then.)
Future Perfect Continuous	*Ma*hangpan *pa*	*Mahangpan pa* nakon ang paathag. (I *will have been understading* the explanation.)

94. To use: gamit

Tenses	Word	Examples
Past Simple	*Nag*gamit	*Naggamit* ako sang mga bulig sa pagtuon. (I *used* study tools.)
Past Continuous	*Nag*gamit	*Naggamit* ako sang mga bulig sa pagtuon. (I *was using* study tools.)
Past Perfect Simple	*Nag*gamit *na*	*Naggamit na* ako sang mga bulig sa pagtuon. (I *had used* study tools.)
Past Perfect Continuous	*Nag*gamit *pa*	*Naggamit pa* ako sang mga bulig sa pagtuon. (I *had been using* study tools.)
Present Simple	*Naga*gamit	*Nagagamit* ako sang mga bulig sa pagtuon. (I *use* study tools.)
Present Continuous	*Naga*gamit	*Nagagamit* ako sang mga bulig sa pagtuon. (I *am using* study tools.)
Present Perfect Simple	*Naga*gamit *na*	*Nagagamit na* ako sang mga bulig sa pagtuon. (I *have used* study tools.)
Present Perfect Continuous	*Naga*gamit *pa*	*Nagagamit pa* ako sang mga bulig sa pagtuon. (I *have been using* study tools.)
Future Simple	*Maga*gamit	*Magagamit* ako sang mga bulig sa pagtuon. (I *will use* study tools.)
Future Continuous	*Maga*gamit	*Magagamit* ako sang mga bulig sa pagtuon. (I *will be using* study tools.)
Future Perfect Simple	*Maga*gamit *na*	*Magagamit na* kuntani ako sang mga bulig sa pagtuon. (I *will have used* study tools by then.)
Future Perfect Continuous	*Maga*gamit *pa*	*Magagamit pa* ako sang mga bulig sa pagtuon. (I *will have been using* study tools.)

95. To wait: hulat

Tenses	Word	Examples
Past Simple	*Nag*hulat	*Naghulat* ako sa imo. (I *waited* for you.)
Past Continuous	*Nag*hulat	*Naghulat* ako sa imo. (I *was waiting* for you.)
Past Perfect Simple	*Nag*hulat *na*	*Naghulat na* ako sa imo. (I *had waited* for you.)
Past Perfect Continuous	*Nag*hulat *pa*	*Naghulat pa* ako sa imo. (I *had been waiting* for you.)
Present Simple	*Naga*hulat	*Nagahulat* ako sa imo. (I *wait* for you.)
Present Continuous	*Naga*hulat	*Nagahulat* ako sa imo. (I *am waiting* for you.)
Present Perfect Simple	*Naga*hulat *na*	*Nagahulat na* ako sa imo. (I *have waited* for you.)
Present Perfect Continuous	*Naga*hulat *pa*	*Nagahulat pa* ako sa imo. (I *have been waiting* for you.)
Future Simple	*Maga*hulat	*Magahulat* ako sa imo. (I *will wait* for you.)
Future Continuous	*Maga*hulat	*Magahulat* ako sa imo. (I *will be waiting* for you.)
Future Perfect Simple	*Maga*hulat *na*	*Magahulat na* kuntani ako sa imo. (I *will have waited* for you by then.)
Future Perfect Continuous	*Maga*hulat *pa*	*Magahulat pa* ako sa imo. (I *will have been waiting* for you.)

96. To walk: lakat

Tenses	Word	Examples
Past Simple	*Nag*lakat	*Naglakat* sia sa husto nga dalan. (She *walked* in the right path.)
Past Continuous	*Nag*lakat	*Naglakat* sia sa husto nga dalan. (She *was walking* in the right path.)
Past Perfect Simple	*Nag*lakat *na*	*Naglakat na* sia sa husto nga dalan. (She *had walked* in the right path.)
Past Perfect Continuous	*Nag*lakat *pa*	*Naglakat pa* sia sa husto nga dalan. (She *had been walking* in the right path.)
Present Simple	*Naga*lakat	*Nagalakat* sia sa husto nga dalan. (She *walks* in the right path.)
Present Continuous	*Naga*lakat	*Nagalakat* sia sa husto nga dalan. (She *is walking* in the right path.)
Present Perfect Simple	*Naga*lakat *na*	*Nagalakat na* sia sa husto nga dalan. (She *has walked* in the right path.)
Present Perfect Continuous	*Naga*lakat *pa*	*Nagalakat pa* sia sa husto nga dalan. (She *has been walking* in the right path.)
Future Simple	*Maga*lakat	*Magalakat* sia sa husto nga dalan. (She *will walk* in the right path.)
Future Continuous	*Maga*lakat	*Magalakat* sia sa husto nga dalan. (She *will be walking* in the right path.)
Future Perfect Simple	*Maga*lakat *na*	*Magalakat na* kuntani sia sa husto nga dalan. (She *will have walked* in the right path by then.)
Future Perfect Continuous	*Maga*lakat *pa*	*Magalakat pa* sia sa husto nga dalan. (She *will have been walking* in the right path.)

97. To want: gusto, gustuhan

Tenses	Word	Examples
Past Simple	_Na_gustuhan	Amo ini ang _nagustuhan_ ko nga kolor sang akon salakyan. (I _wanted_ my car this colour.)
Past Continuous	No equivalent	No equivalent
Past Perfect Simple	No equivalent	No equivalent
Past Perfect Continuous	No equivalent	No equivalent
Present Simple	gusto	Amo ini ang _gusto_ ko nga kolor sang akon salakyan. (I _want_ my car this colour.)
Present Continuous	No equivalent	No equivalent
Present Perfect Simple	No equivalent	No equivalent
Present Perfect Continuous	No equivalent	No equivalent
Future Simple	No equivalent	No equivalent
Future Continuous	No equivalent	No equivalent
Future Perfect Simple	No equivalent	No equivalent
Future Perfect Continuous	No equivalent	No equivalent

98. To watch: tan-aw

Tenses	Word	Examples
Past Simple	*Nag*tan-aw	*Nagtan-aw* sila sang sine. (They *watched* movie.)
Past Continuous	*Nag*tan-aw	*Nagtan-aw* sila sang sine. (They *were watching* movie.)
Past Perfect Simple	*Nag*tan-aw *na*	*Nagtan-aw na* sila sang sine. (They *had watched* movie.)
Past Perfect Continuous	*Nag*tan-aw *pa*	*Nagtan-aw pa* sila sang sine. (They *had been watching* movie.)
Present Simple	*Naga*tan-aw	*Nagatan-aw* sila sang sine. (They *watch* movie.)
Present Continuous	*Naga*tan-aw	*Nagatan-aw* sila sang sine. (They *are watching* movie.)
Present Perfect Simple	*Naga*tan-aw *na*	*Nagatan-aw na* sila sang sine. (They *have watched* movie.)
Present Perfect Continuous	*Naga*tan-aw *pa*	*Nagatan-aw pa* sila sang sine. (They *have been watching* movie.)
Future Simple	*Maga*tan-aw	*Magatan-aw* sila sang sine. (They *will watch* movie.)
Future Continuous	*Maga*tan-aw	*Magatan-aw* sila sang sine. (They *will be watching* movie.)
Future Perfect Simple	*Maga*tan-aw *na*	*Magatan-aw na* kuntani sila sang sine. (They *will have watched* movie by then.)
Future Perfect Continuous	*Maga*tan-aw *pa*	*Magatan-aw pa* sila sang sine. (They *will have been watching* movie.)

99. To win: daog

Tenses	Word	Examples
Past Simple	**Nag**daog	*Nagdaog* sia sa hampang. (He *won* the game.)
Past Continuous	**Nag**daog	*Nagdaog* sia sa hampang. (He *was winning* the game.)
Past Perfect Simple	**Nag**daog **na**	*Nagdaog na* sia sa hampang. (He *had won* the game.)
Past Perfect Continuous	**Nag**daog **pa**	*Nagdaog pa* sia sa hampang. (He *had been winning* the game.)
Present Simple	**Naga**daog	*Nagadaog* sia sa hampang. (He *wins* the game.)
Present Continuous	**Naga**daog	*Nagadaog* sia sa hampang. (He *is winning* the game.)
Present Perfect Simple	**Naga**daog **na**	*Nagadaog na* sia sa hampang. (He *has won* the game.)
Present Perfect Continuous	**Naga**daog **pa**	*Nagadaog pa* sia sa hampang. (He *has been winning* the game.)
Future Simple	**Maga**daog	*Magadaog* sia sa hampang. (He *will win* the game.)
Future Continuous	**Maga**daog	*Magadaog* sia sa hampang. (He *will be winning* the game.)
Future Perfect Simple	**Maga**daog **na**	*Magadaog na* kuntani sia sa hampang. (He *will have won* the game by then.)
Future Perfect Continuous	**Maga**daog **pa**	*Magadaog pa* sia sa hampang. (He *will have been winning* the game.)

100. To work: obra

Tenses	Word	Examples
Past Simple	*Nag*-obra	*Nag-obra* ako sing maayo. (I *worked* well.)
Past Continuous	*Nag*-obra	*Nag-obra* ako sing maayo. (I *was working* well.)
Past Perfect Simple	*Nag*-obra *na*	*Nag-obra na* ako sing maayo. (I *had worked* well.)
Past Perfect Continuous	*Nag*-obra *pa*	*Nag-obra pa* ako sing maayo. (I *had been working* well.)
Present Simple	*Naga*obra	*Nagaobra* ako sing maayo. (I *work* well.)
Present Continuous	*Naga*obra	*Nagaobra* ako sing maayo. (I *am working* well.)
Present Perfect Simple	*Naga*obra *na*	*Nagaobra na* ako sing maayo. (I *have worked* well.)
Present Perfect Continuous	*Naga*obra *pa*	*Nagaobra pa* ako sing maayo. (I *have been working* well.)
Future Simple	*Maga*obra	*Magaobra* ako sing maayo. (I *will work* well.)
Future Continuous	*Maga*obra	*Magaobra* ako sing maayo. (I *will be working* well.)
Future Perfect Simple	*Maga*obra *na*	*Magaobra na* kuntani ako sing maayo. (I *will have worked* well by then.)
Future Perfect Continuous	*Maga*obra *pa*	*Magaobra pa* ako sing maayo. (I *will have been working* well.)

101. To write: sulat

Tenses	Word	Examples
Past Simple	*Nag*sulat	*Nagsulat* sia sa akon. (She *wrote* to me.)
Past Continuous	*Nag*sulat	*Nagsulat* sia sa akon. (She *was writing* to me.)
Past Perfect Simple	*Nag*sulat *na*	*Nagsulat na* sia sa akon. (She *had wrote* to me.)
Past Perfect Continuous	*Nag*sulat *pa*	*Nagsulat pa* sia sa akon. (She *had been writing* to me.)
Present Simple	*Naga*sulat	*Nagasulat* sia sa akon. (She *writes* to me.)
Present Continuous	*Naga*sulat	*Nagasulat* sia sa akon. (She *is writing* to me.)
Present Perfect Simple	*Naga*sulat *na*	*Nagasulat na* sia sa akon. (She *has written* to me.)
Present Perfect Continuous	*Naga*sulat *pa*	*Nagasulat pa* sia sa akon. (She *has been writing* to me.)
Future Simple	*Maga*sulat	*Magasulat* sia sa akon. (She *will write* to me.)
Future Continuous	*Maga*sulat	*Magasulat* sia sa akon. (She *will be writing* to me.)
Future Perfect Simple	*Maga*sulat *na*	*Magasulat na* kuntani sia sa akon. (She *will have written* to me by then.)
Future Perfect Continuous	*Maga*sulat *pa*	*Magasulat pa* sia sa akon. (She *will have been writing* to me.)

Made in the USA
Coppell, TX
01 November 2020